THE CREATIVE ETHERS

RONALD BEESLEY

The Creative Ethers

LONDON

NEVILLE SPEARMAN

First published in Great Britain in 1975 by
Neville Spearman Limited
112 Whitfield Street, London W1P 6DP

© Ronald Beesley 1975

ISBN 0 85435 472 7

Set in 11/13 pt Juliana and Printed by
Clarke, Doble & Brendon Ltd., Plymouth
using Caxton a/w paper supplied by
Frank Grunfeld Ltd., London
Bound by G. & J. Kitcat Ltd., London

CONTENTS

PART ONE

The Creative Ethers

CHAPTER ONE

The Creative Ethers

The creative ethers are the substances—the materials of the Cosmic workshop and it is here we begin to study the basic functions and systems of order by and through which the Universe keeps in motion and creativeness, fertility, form, shape, colour and so on. As we deal with these different manifestations of the life-force, bear in mind that at first it may appear indiscriminate, for the threads will not be drawn together until we get nearer the end of this particular part of our study.

Many people are not aware that the creative principle in life is the texture of thought-flow which welds itself into what we term the free ethers the free gases—which are in different substances or levels. These different energies have frequencies, every one of which has a certain wavelength. There are seven major wavelength circuits of the higher ethers which are manifesting in the world today; each of these represents one of the seven spheres which manifest from The Christ Source to the third-dimensional one which we occupy.

It is possible through thought-projection to mould the shape and texture of these particular etheric forces, and combine them into life patterns or sequences of events, once we realize that we are dealing with malleable matters.

The substance of life which surrounds us is also malleable, and vital in that it has energies of its own. This is important, otherwise our status, our manifestation, our investigation, within the forces of science and nature would not be completely whole, but would be distorted and diffused. The various worlds of metal, minerals and various levels of ether, are a combination of the free gases, some blended by the efforts of man either in the workshop or the laboratory and woven into the fabric of our civilization.

Thus we are drawing in not merely metals and minerals, but the substance of the ethers which creates these forms, or supplies them with their adhesion and vitality.

Now vitality and the ethers are close together. We are already aware that things will fatigue—that metal will fatigue as will our bodies—and it is where these ether combinations or vitalities become dispersed that we have a breakdown of a life pattern. We are witnessing this by way of atomic explosions at the moment. These release forces into the ethers surrounding our Planet, causing them to become higher in radio activity than the normal balance will allow. We see the results of this imbalance in the disturbance of the weather patterns and the seasons, and the radiation belt. It will also affect the Cosmic and Solar Rays, for the balance of these ethers is so interwoven that one reacts upon the others. Try to see this great scale of evolution creating worlds within worlds, creating patterns of colour, sound and form, all of them moulded by the procedure of thought—that is, the power and texture of Supreme Mind.

The Universe is Mind in action, and each Planet, each part of these particular variations combine to make a whole. The Astrologers are not far out when they speak of influences and variations and pressures which come to bear on a life-force at given times or periods, within the wavelength with which that life-force is interwoven. Although we can study this from the astrological point of view, we can also study it from the metaphysical aspect and take it much further.

In our life pattern, that is, the individual world we have partially created, we manifest the shape of our bodies, the colour of our skin, we manifest within ourselves, balance or imbalance. We can, and do, generate certain currents, streams and forces—in other words, we are using or welding together the various ether forces within the life-force of ourselves and creating atmospheres, climates and all we need.

10

Christian Scientists have this idea in their doctrine of mind over matter. There is some truth in this in that mind in the creative ethers is the stuff of which worlds are made.

This begins to open up new channels by which we can combine our thinking with directive purpose. We find that the degree of energy or health is decided by the state of purpose or motive of the individual. Thus, if we have a purpose, we form a plan of unfoldment, a system by which we can live; but if there is no plan or system, no unfoldment or purpose, then the creative patterns within that life-force become unattached to the point they can even be an alien force within the body itself. Should we find alien energies exerting a pressure within the human body, it is fair to suspect that the mind forces are at variance or emotional influences are undermining them. Mind is a state of health and the non-use or right use of latent forces determines the life balance. This removes the idea of anything being immovable or incurable. What has happened can 'un-happen'; when the force involved has been re-directed by another thought texture, the situation will change, provided the personality allows it.

Now, the ego or personality and the thought life are so woven together that sometimes it is difficult to know where one begins and the other ends; but we are dealing with different structures, some temporary, others more permanent, we can experiment with our creativeness and discover by trial and error, the varying results of our applications. Our Earth life is really an experiment in creativeness. Our bodies are our personal representation of work done, in which we are expressing our personality, through the mind, creating or helping the shape of things to come and blending our outer and inner life, putting into action our dreams and desires. Up to now most of this work has been done on the unconscious plane, and has not reached recognition at a conscious level, with the result that we have created haphazardly and often unwisely. Very often we have reflected into the body the denser ethers when we should have been creating with the higher ones. The denser ethers are known as the electric and magnetic fields; they are a part of the gravity of this Planet. They also represent the heavy minerals, lead, iron and the lower forms of rock structure. In other words, the density of the lower ethers performs the functions of weight and force, in the lowest part of the Planetary life. If we study the occult aspects of arsenic, lead, iron, tin, gold and copper, we find that these substances are wavelengths in ether—that is, they are wavelengths of substances we recognize as minerals. But bear in mind that these minerals already exist within the etheric pattern and can be drawn from that source into a substance or shape.

This may be difficult to understand, but one day we shall know more about these sciences, in that we shall be able to draw from the creative ethers direct, all the gold, copper, silver, iron or tin that we require, because such resources already exist on a plane above, and what we see of them in the earth is the lower manifestation of them in Time. This is exciting because it shows that what we think of as solidity and weight no longer has that bearing. The Alchemist of old dreamed of producing gold from lead, but had he studied the higher Alchemy of how to harness the creative ethers, he might have had more success. We have used the words before—"As above so below." We have no substance in the lower which does not already exist in a higher form, or ether; and so the stratas build up and up into the great Etheric Worlds where Light becomes the form of substance, not matter as we know it here.

Now to understand that the etheric forces of Light are the means by which all other life forces are moulded or controlled may be difficult, but try to picture living in a black and white world with no apparent Sun. We immediately recognize that Light itself is not only a form of Solar or Cosmic fuel which the body is using to absorb and reabsorb life, but the actual radiation of the Solar forces relying upon the flow of creative ethers to distribute its right food, stimulation and subsequent energies. The same applies to the gases of the air and the water we drink. These are creative ethers in flow each having its own level of service, each contributing to the overall pattern of life as we know it; such take on shape and form, perpetuating and

12

feeding the life principle. What I am trying to convey and explain are the many layers of creativity which exist over and above the World we know. We think of our World as sentient, the earth we walk on, the things we feel and hear, the substance and shape of things we see, but this is only a world of shadow. It is not a world of pure Reality. It is formed of a lower creative substance made especially to be moulded and directed by the human mind and utilized by the primitive forces of nature, raising it into a higher vibrating substance, enlarging the conscious state and developing the mind.

Knowing this helps the elasticity of our minds to come to our rescue. Though to many this world is Reality, the Esoterics refer to it as the world of Illusion, but I would rather you sensed it as the world of Experimentation. It is not a world of finality, nor is it completion. Many things thought of by man do not exist in the pure creative ethers; they exist in the peculiar texture of man's thinking. The different states between Heaven and Earth are mind manifestations, striving to activate on a higher plane of creativeness, thereby releasing new forces.

We are already aware of the atomic forces which surround us, but these, although complex, are a primitive range. They occupy very low levels in the energy fertility of the Universe. By energy fertility, I am referring to the sources of perpetual motion which penetrate and activate these fields as they penetrate many others before they reach the very lowest planes of primeval energies. Mankind is at the cross-roads of his evolution. We have reason to believe that surges flow in threes and that seven is the cycle of Soul liberation. So, should we have been through three Planetary stages in reaching the Earth, we evolve through those stages to be released from the Earth. This, then, is the cross-roads in Time and a pure experiment in living.

In therapeutic work we notice that much of the involvement of ill health is due to the intake of the denser ethers which have been manifested into the force of this life, as also in other lives. We all know that if a material is unbalanced it is not dependable. It will fracture, break or fatigue easily and erode more quickly. This can happen in body manifestation. Incompatible

13

substances have been drawn into the body, also woven into the texture of the mind, which are not for us. In other words, illness is an experiment which has gone into excess and needs correction.

It is possible through using the higher awareness of the consciousness, to utilize a new creative level, to weave into the instinctive life around us a new vitality, a new fertility. If we look for the essentials of evolution we must look upwards, not downwards. Manifest upwards, not downwards.

Therefore the bodies of the future can be enhanced by the right use of today, but we are interested at the moment in our personal manifestation of the creative ethers; these we have seen as substances in our body and our health pattern. As we are able to visualize that there exists a new vitality and higher ether creation, where other levels of creative ethers can superimpose themselves upon a lower, and improve, purify, cleanse and strengthen it, we begin to see that there is a new power open to humanity to change its life, its ways, its systems, that there is a new personality potential and that this force can be rewoven into the body fabric here and now.

Mind and matter are closely associated, therefore our thinking force will instil into the body texture the thought wavelength by which we decide to live. The past and present do show, but when we release the spiritual personality from the mind, then the creative ethers are also quickly released, and this new vitality begins to flow again. A strange thing, is this new creative ether. At first the ailments seem worse than they were before; the aches appear to increase, and a state of irregularity to exist while changing from one wavelength or vibration to another. Not knowing of this is why some people say it is dangerous to 'play' with these things. But we may as well say it is dangerous to use electricity—keep to candles! This transfer period whereby the conscious vibrations of the body remanifest themselves, is a very exciting thing. At the same time it is highly sensitive. As we release ourselves from the denser ethers and their pattern and begin to know what freedom of life really means, it is quite exhilarating to realize and feel our perspectives quickening and know that we are tuned in to new mental thinking. This is digging deep because we now realize that the key to this new world has been here all the time, locked up in our spiritual personality.

We, as seekers, should know more about these creative ethers, also more about levitation. We should begin to know how it is possible that we could walk on water, how eventually become free from the drag-chains of gravity, and live and move by thought and not be limited to the denser ethers through which we have lived, and which we have accepted as natural. Man has sunk into and seemed akin to the denser ethers, but he should not have done so. It is a retrogression of his evolutionary pattern, where he has allowed the primal sources of his instinctive nature to over-run, and sacrificed his intuitional and spiritual resources in the process.

But now we have a way back. Man has to learn from the science of his thinking life not to turn to chemicals for his salvation, to drugs by which the body is suppressed. We have to teach the personality mind to reach a new substance, and from that be able to strengthen, cleanse and refashion the form we already have, and also begin the preparation for an entirely new body which we shall be occupying very soon. This is the one we will use on our next evolutionary stage. We are forming the stages and textures by the way we think, live and manifest now. So it is not just a question of keeping the body free from pain, and having the vitality to do the things we want to do. This force and power is over and above these things and exists on a higher level, but it can be drawn upon and shaped into new forms.

This is the basis of etheric healing. In this manner the consciousness of the individual who is able to reach to these creative levels, can draw down this power into the life-force of the person needing help and set in motion a new rhythm, a new level of manifestation, by providing new patterns, new impetus. This material has been likened to spiritual yeast which provides the over-used body with a new vitality which it was unable to do for itself. Such is etheric medicine, which is based on drawing down on the higher creative ethers to correct the primitive lower ones. This is not only a redemption from error, but it is the eternal promise of life more abundant. We can bring about this etheric change of health pattern here and reap its benefits on another plane. Many on arrival at their next stage have been surprised at the work done—others whose forces are more dense in the primitive ethers, find that to raise them above that level means long and arduous work. Some, as if by a touch of magic, become infused with the new material almost instantly. The life-force itself seems to reach into another plane of activity and the whole personality appears changed, they are now vibrating, feeding and living from a higher etheric force than the one which made them sad and depleted before.

An important study is the consciousness at these levels. We cannot just ignore them or sing hymns about them. We must, as learners in the great field of life, enter further into them as seekers and activators, and begin to draw down this life-force into an impoverished soul-hungry world, to the many who live in it who are bored, empty and unhappy, and whose future has lost its purpose and direction; they are seeking soul-satisfaction at the lower primitive levels to which they do not really belong.

Therefore, by raising the consciousness out of the material role, and seeking to instruct the subconscious mind into new levels in which it can reform and lead them into hitherto unknown fields, we can help people to draw for themselves upon this substance to such a measure that there is no limit except the lack of mind and will. So, to quicken the mind and Spirit is the answer to these problems, and it is through Spirit, via the mind, that the Soul is able to bring forth its higher pattern and creativeness—which is not only a power to heal but to re-manifest the life force itself. Even if only a few people think on these lines, it enables this new environment to penetrate into our generation, beginning as a new zest, a fresh level of thinking vitality by which mankind can be raised from the doldrums and sterilities of his lower senses, and eventually released into the higher patterns where he belongs.

16

The concentration on medicine today makes it the second largest industry in the world, next to armaments, but if we are to discover a new road to health and other levels of thinking, we shall not find it through massive drugs or suppressive therapies. Unless we can reach out to these other creative etheric sources and draw them into the substance of health and living, there is no permanent answer to man's health problem. We may not be able to release this new pattern at once, but these things will be known and recognized by the work they do.

As each begins to get this idea we can see that man is living and existing below his true level in the Universe. His future is not in the hands of politicians, religions or the Welfare State, but in the mind/spirit relationship of each individual person. This is where our work must lie, by stimulating this new field of thinking on to another level of sensitivity, releasing it, not only in health patterns but in all the systems whereby man lives, and eventually by bringing forth this higher manifesting material, make it possible to build a new world.

By our misuse of nature's resources we have created a fear-ridden, unhappy world, ever on the edge of war. This primitive force which is being drawn back again through man's politics and behaviour is a force which should have left our world long ago. It is a retrogression, back to the dark forces from which man has already risen and, therefore, his place in the Planetary culture should be above what it is now, and be supreme; it can be, if we can draw this new material and substance again into our daily thinking. This is not a dream of 'pie in the sky'. It is not some glorious paradise hereafter. This is work, real work, here and now, for merely to live a life of sense perception and not, by our thinking, raise the values of our time, is to deny the reason of our coming. But, finally, life is the call of the Spirit. It is a call to other higher recognitions. It is a lifting out from the hopelessness of human poverty, to release into life a new vitality and meaning. It is immaterial to what age group we belong for it is the personality that counts. There is no such thing as age on the evolutionary path—there are but degrees of awakened maturity, and in this maturity of Spirit, the emergence of spiritual awakening, each has a big part to play. In discussion, and bringing these things forward as basic ideas and thoughts, we begin to get through the density of these primitive ethers and raise them up into a lighter one, strengthening, purifying and releasing the pattern in which we are at this moment deeply immersed and pathetically living. So healing is for the world in ideas, and not only healing of the personality and the body. Get this wider concept and you will find that it becomes both exciting and moving, because it is reaching into the memory depths, trying to stir up what we already know; reaching out to a new horizon, to bring back fresh vitality, new concepts, new powers, new forces, which are waiting on man's awakening, for every one to use. By thinking on these wavelengths you will be bringing into action a new relationship, a purpose, a meaning which is so desperately needed by your fellow human beings whose senses are drugged and who are miserable in their darkness. This is work, a challenge. So let us commence our new living on a practical, spiritual and natural level.

MEDITATION

Reach out into this world of GOD'S practical
Reality, into the Spiritual resources, realizing
the Divine urge behind every human life to
reach out to perfection which, although it does
not yet know, it yearns for with all its intensity, all its heart and all its Spirit.

CHAPTER TWO

Vibrations—Rhythms—Laws

In speaking of the vibrations and Rhythms of the Ray forces of the Cosmos—we are dealing with fundamental science in an interdimensional way. Spiritual science has known for many years of the existence of these waves of matter. Material science is beginning to discover that matter is not only inert, dense substance, but is a series of waves in motion. We are living by and through the oscillation of these great waves which have their origin far beyond space. In these waves we have the formation of light, colour and energy, controlled responses, controlled groupings, controlled rhythms.

The fascinating thing is, that when dealing with formations of vibrations which reach the Earth from outer space—with which forces the Earth is in a state of receptivity—we find the centre by which these vibrations exist has a certain key in the human heart. These vibrations possess a form of personality, and have definite mental links as well as spiritual form. They contain substance in an energized, controlled force which centres round the human body and life, feeding its inner consciousness or inner life-force. We, as seekers for the occult truth, are more concerned with the unseen life-forces than with those which we see. We are well aware of the body we can feel, of the life we expect, but few are sufficiently aware of the life-force which is concealed—that is, the life-force behind the human pattern. It is in this life-force that we find the true potential of the nature of the human Being, wherein is concealed the data and blue print of the person, the invisible life power, that which is the substance of the life and the controlling information. We are enclosed so much within the physical body that we scarcely live at all. The human body is not a truly intelligent life-force and has no permanent state, but it has enough force to motivate the mind and be immersed into the denser waves of Planetary life; it is only a dependant and owes its existence to a life-force exterior to its own. We are accustomed to the words 'Man liveth not by bread alone' but what we may not have realized is that the great vibrational resources of the Cosmos feed the mind and the soul, and the intermediate "dual personality" also.

Now, dual personality is something we must get accustomed to, because it will cause us our greatest difficulty in unfulfilment. We are so many things and personalities at different times, changing every minute of the day, that our relationship to each other is guided and shaped entirely by what we call reflection, which is a vibration of personality, one between the other. If we like a person then that part of our personality will vibrate towards them at a higher note; if we dislike, then it will cause a lower vibration. Each of the intermediate patterns of human behaviour have their reflection in vibratory existence, and in the interaction of one personality upon another we have the overall pattern of human behaviour.

To be free from the negative density of human relations of vibratory matter needs tremendous work and self-discipline— not to be influenced by these external vibratory waves but keep our individuality free from immersion into the vibratory substances. In simple words, if we have bad-tempered people around us, do not become bad-tempered too; if we have impatient, discontented people, we must watch that we do not allow that vibratory reflection to cause us to be the same.

So easily can these emotional, vibrations be exchanged that in war we find nice people doing terrible things because the vibrational influence is compelling them to act in that unfortunate way. We are much more aware of our negative state, because this oscillates slowly and is therefore more apparent to us than our higher state.

Thus the vibrational reflection between personalities is a

form of communication which will retaliate or encourage, nourish or deplete it, according to the vibratory density and its force.

Bear in mind the fact that we could not live without the vibratory reflection, that the whole Universe would become out of sequence in time, and orderliness would go if this should cease. Orderliness, or controlled waves of matter from a higher dimension exercise pressure upon the lower dimension and act as a Cosmic rein, to keep sequence within this vibrational matter. This we must accept as a form of density in which the higher operational laws command and feed into the lower set of laws, this sequence within time. If we understood this a little more we should find we could supersede all illness and death; we should know how to select a wavelength to find this vibratory substance of the life force which can be received in such a way that our operative energies are kept at a high rate of efficiency. In fact, to live efficiently is to live in a receptive way. We know when that wave is operative because we are happy, in tune, in step, in flow—this free power is called by many names—then we live in a heaven, entirely different from the monotonous experience of being out of step with everybody.

But the student on the Path must realize this is the natural way to live, to be within the harmonious wavelength when the Spirit vibrates with the energy substance of matter, which becomes our servant and carries us through the day, and saves not only our physical resources, but is profitable to us in what we call the sequence of time. To understand this we must pass on to the rhythm of flow, for each is in a constant state of perpetual motion. Once we realize that the time factor of the wavelength gives us a new centre, the next step is to keep within the state of rhythm, the harmonious flow, which controls the seasons by the movement of the Planet and is part of the great Cosmic outflow which multiplies itself in sequence and in form.

If we knew more about this, we should not be so concerned with crime and crises and their effects, but realize that the harmonious rhythms are the factors by which we progress, and they enable us to live within events, and what are events but Cosmic Laws operating within time? Every event has a key within a key; all events are timed outside matter. Each experience we meet is participating in an event, though that event may be in another part of the world, in another language or dimension; but as this sequence of events unfolds within the rhythm of time, so are the great forces released which serve and feed those events.

You have noticed that some days you are in step with time. Whatever you do seems to be in step, so that your train or bus arrangements for a journey, your appointment, the book you read, the food you have—everything comes into flow with what we call the rhythm of events. A greater understanding of prophecy would allow us to forecast the turn of events, because events are the climate in which we live. If we are in tune with events, in time with Time, fulfilling ourselves as within experience, then we heighten the whole purpose of life by raising it to a higher density level.

Astrology has, perhaps, done its best to reach into the rhythm of events; using the Stars as a means of calculation, with Sun and Moon in their different ways oscillating in space, man has tried to decipher the key to events. We should realize that life can be lived in harmonious flow. We are already aware of the wavelength supply, now we have to be in time with all things, all life.

It is said that the Cosmic memory can take the place of human memory. I have seen this happen—people able to tell the time and date, without any physical means of knowing. Swedenborg used this to reach into events thousands of miles away. He described a burning city in another country, at a time when there was no form of communication except by word of mouth. He could instantly report happenings which were taking place in the sequence of time. Now Swedenborg had touched this key, so the event became physically pictorial to his vision, enabling him to record the complete detailed information. We cannot all be Swedenborgs but, as students of this philosophy, we realize that this has to do with us also not only in our daily living, but in as much as we should seek to improve our reception of these vibrations. First we must realize that these events have already happened, though it is difficult to appreciate that we live in a time-delay density. We find spiritual science tells of the power of prophecy and most religions include it—also it formed a natural part in the Christian, Jewish and Ancient histories.

But now we see these things, not as part of religion but as something that affects us personally. We can raise the frequency of our life-force by utilizing these natural resources. We may not be able to do it by extra-sensory means, or by applied insight, because it is more or less a rhythm. To start harmonizing this, the first thing to do is to 'feel' your day because this day has already happened. It is now going to unfold itself in your life. Therefore, before you cast yourself on the events of the day, reach out to it, feel for it, sense it, and try to get its communication.

You may feel it is a day for a journey or meeting or a day to just keep quiet. When the energy factor is high you are aware of it, because you achieve an enormous amount in that day with very little expenditure of energy. Your personal life is in rhythm with time, with the events taking place, not only throughout the entire world, but throughout the Cosmos.

I know a traveller who is a very fine seeker on the Path, and we discussed this rhythm of events in application to industry and commerce; he thought it could be used more for the normal everyday happenings affecting the family to use events within the Rhythms of time and utilize life more effectively. So he tried experimenting, with results which were rather unusual. He was not a lazy man but sometimes felt he should stay at home and write letters. His employer thought him a little odd, but the extraordinary thing was that at the end of twelve months his record of sales was the highest in the firm and his total mileage the lowest they had ever recorded. His visits were fewer and yet more profitable, and his ideas put into action were the most successful because they were in tune with time and events. Some said he was practising black magic on the customers! There are always people who are ready to so describe anything which has some supernormal activity to it. But there is nothing supernormal in this. If we accept the prophecies of the Old and New Testaments we must accept this as a modern scientific fact emerging in a new form of human response connected with the spiritual idea. It is not that we should use this for gain, but it would be pointless to make journeys and find people out or not in a mood to talk business, or what we wanted to talk about could not be discussed at that time because the fulfilment of the event was incomplete. Therefore prophecy is the normal answer, and can be used in a realistic way in our everyday activities and communications.

The next theme for study is the mechanics or mathematics of our living and this we apply in terms of race. This can mean race Karma, culture, types of art and literature, but what we should be more aware of is that the life-force pattern supplies special knowledge which is communicable to certain groups or types.

As we begin to understand group law, we find that all species whether birds, fish, plants or human beings, depend upon a permanent flow of power or knowledge. If we interfere or create a barrier between this energy-ray flow and the group which it is feeding by controlling or instructing it and keeping it within its normal rhythm, it's communications break down and the results are disastrous.

A friend of mine who kept pigeons was curious as to why pigeons always returned home, why swallows use the same building for nesting. He found that when radar was introduced his pigeons did not come home so well—indeed many strange things happened in connection with the life of the birds because there was interference with the informative ray which links them; it appeared in some way disturbed, the communication was delayed and so the bird lost its sense of direction and became quite inefficient. So, my friend said, "If I can put a radar screen around the loft and increase the magnetic field by which pigeons work, it may help them." And sure enough the pigeons came home.

The point was that he increased the magnetic field in what was called the homing zone. This Ray force is the means by which birds travel over vast distances from the Continent and back, provided the homing ray is not interfered with. The pressures that make salmon go up rivers to spawn are also in the control of this force. But we must bear in mind that we are each different—we have evolved out of the group and so are not controlled in the same way through the instincts. The bird knows how to build its nest, what type of food to eat, when to breed and when not. It is informed from the moment it breaks out of its shell; it knows its pattern of life without any training or instruction. It comes under the information of the Ray that looks after that particular species and the behaviour within that pattern goes on in a controlled and orderly way. That is a very wonderful thing. We take it for granted, but when we think of the schooling we have to go through even to go out and come in, how hardly in fact we acquire our basic knowledge! But the personality must evolve through its own development: we cannot have everything laid down for us from the start to the finish. We must at some time take on the responsibility ourselves, and it is an important moment when we are able for the first time to receive our particular wave-force. Our nature, our type, our group, and our entire personality decides our wavelength, and what feeds one will not necessarily feed another. There are as many variations in the subtle forces of the human personality as there are people, and each is completely different. Just as your fingerprints are different from anybody else's so is your Ray communication linked to you only, and the path in which you are being led and instructed. Think of your fingerprints and your personal Ray force. If you can attune your personality to your supply line, you will have health, energy, a sense of rhythm, motion, efficiency and being quite beyond anything we normally know. The only thing which can interfere with the particular Ray force is the human mind and personality, and instead of entering as a straight flow into the great centres of the heart and mind, it becomes dispersed, making us dense and unguided, and difficult to reach. In therapeutic work we find, in many instances, that what people need is to be re-established in their own natural wavelength. Often if that is re-polarized, it is sufficient to restore health. They begin to take on a new lease of life, to resume their natural temperament and character.

If we allow ourselves to go down into the misery, despondency and negativeness of human nature at its worst, we create an etheric condition, a miasma into which the life-force cannot reach. It cannot penetrate this darkness, this density we have allowed to form, thus we lose all sense of higher dimensional activity and are over-immersed in the human density atmosphere. This makes us accident-prone, unable to concentrate; our sense of proportion gets out of focus, and we are out of tune with ourselves. The answer is to stop and reason with this thing and say, "I am out of tune with my individual Ray force to the great GOD force, so I will indraw to reconnect myself." Only then can you become re-charged, re-vitalized—and life becomes in tune. If you cannot do it for yourself seek out one who can. Those of you who have experienced esoteric healing and are familiar with the soft glow, the sense of healing, the new happiness and power, will know to what I am referring.

This is not only a time for praying, it is also a time for self-work. This is the mechanical part of esoteric work, where the student is taught a sense of responsibility to the invisible pattern of life, to begin to use these things in a new way. By utilizing them within ourselves we help other people to utilize their own potential.

Now this is the test—to be able to keep within our own Ray rhythm when the world around is disorganized and sad, to maintain a sense of communication in the midst of chaos and doubt, fear and uncertainty. If we can, we will find our lifeline will also feed others through our nourishment, environment and personality, until they are strong enough to re-emerge and establish themselves in direct communication with their personal intimate resource.

Here we must become aware of the subtle forces involved. Such time as we feel any fear of life, or death, or of events—and we usually fear the worst—remember, the worst seldom happens. If we remain calm we can often avoid turning a normal event into a disaster. It is a duty to keep cool, calm and quiet and letting the event pass, maintain this communication with the invisible pattern of life; in doing this you will contribute something for the world.

There is a reference in the Bible to a whole city being saved by ten just men. The world can be helped by people realizing the great Cosmic force at work. Acquire this in meditation and self-work, and you will find you know things you never knew before: a wisdom comes beyond ordinary personal experience; a sense of new experience and decision which has nothing to do with human reasoning begins to pervade the whole personality. A sense of active communication will flow into normal everyday affairs, and the productivity and efficiency of life will increase because you are using the natural resources of GOD flowing from the centre of the Cosmos to the outer planes, nourishing the life forces as they were intended to do.

MEDITATION

· Let us enter into the silence with a sense of deep respect that these treasures are ours—we are living in and are part of them; we are, in fact, the purpose of them. Therefore tune in to them and use them wisely.

CHAPTER THREE

Rays—Radiations as Foods

These are the radiations which comprise the different forces of the Cosmic ethers—it is for each of us to realize that natural ethers and currents of energy, influence and affect every personality. They are not something vague and far away. These rays and forces are as close as the air we breathe, the earth we walk on, the sun we feel, and the atmosphere which surrounds us.

The Cosmic and Nature forces are in a continual state of exchange, and in exchanging, each form or Planet radiates into space the state of its Being, the force of its consciousness, and the purpose for which it is contributing to evolution.

We are well aware of the Sun and its contribution to us in the sense of solar currents, solar heat, and the solar resources which help to build up the natural atmosphere as we know it. Therefore, if we can discover the different relationships of Planetary communication, it is easier for us to find a difference between receptivity, transmission, and that which radiates as influence.

We must see the Universe as a power station, each unit of the system having a particular energy part to play in the balance and co-ordination of the whole. We do not live in splendid isolation, but in very close, very intimate association with the Infinite as well as with the finite.

These forces we know as rays or radiations, each ray being a part of a controlling influence and supporting, feeding and maintaining in a creative state, that life which it ensouls and to which it has its affinity. Once we see this, then that affinity to a ray-force encourages us to tune in to our particular food or resources and brings knowledge, information, atmosphere and energy into a state of receptivity.

At our present stage we receive far more than we are able to transmit, and if it were not for those rays everything on earth would decay and substance would have no continuity. Man certainly does not live by bread alone and his substance is entirely dependent upon these exterior forces or radiations to maintain positive patterns of life.

We can recognize this in what we term the five senses. Each sense is a communication and each faculty must be fed. If a faculty is not fed it no longer has any existence, so the more we feed into it, the deeper is its unfoldment and implementation. We develop the physical sense of sight in spaciousness, colour and distance, and in that particular field we derive much enjoyment, for here we have a developed faculty working.

But that faculty can only work as long as it is fed, and as the physical sight is fed by the passing moment, so does the deeper faculty, which we call insight, depend greatly upon a feed-in system whereby it is able to make use of different ray energies which it can transmute into knowledge and information.

The same is true of the sense of hearing and the faculties of touch taste and smell, but these are low in the receptive ray forces, so low that we are hardly aware of their existence. It is true to say that we function only by a higher faculty which, in its turn, activates a lower.

In the psychic field, we know there is a faculty which enables those who possess it to see a fourth-dimensional world and those who inhabit it, and to witness fourth-dimensional phenomena. This so-called "second sight" is far different from physical sight, but those who have this means of perception have to utilize a ray-force or its influence, to feed that information through to the normal consciousness. This supernormal faculty is known in the psychic field as clairvoyance, psychometry, extra-sensory perception, all different forms of sensitivity.

Many people think that this is a most desirable state, but if we rely entirely upon psychic perception—that is, an astral perception or projection—and do not reach out into the higher rays of information, the informative waves or forces, then we are limiting the vision of Soul participation.

Now try to think of these waves as living forces. We are accustomed to think of heat or cold waves, radio and TV waves and light waves. In fact, colour and spectrum waves also have their own wavelength so that the various octaves of colour and energy all operate in known movements; each of these movements follows a definite line or curve, and within the wavelength of each force or energy is contained the ensoulment, in part or complete, of all pre-knowledge, pre-existence, past, present and future. We see further that the Universe is made up of many power houses, Stars and Planets and each of these various stations and Planetary influences is sustaining and feeding certain sections of evolution, and the personality which is involved in that evolution can be receptive to those forces.

We know that in Atlantis, for instance, the gravity wave was well known and utilized as a means of lifting rocks and stones for enormous buildings, whereas today we use great physical energy and mechanical aids to achieve the same ends. It is possible to find the wavelength of all phenomena and, by utilizing it and making use of the fourth-dimensional ray or energy or food—it is all the same—we can then re-manifest within that energy and utilize it as a form of life. This may be easier to explain by electricity. Think of the Earth as a huge dynamo revolving in space. As it revolves it is bathed in all the different radiations of other Planetary systems, Stars and Worlds; it is also ensouled in its own tremendously powerful magnetic field, and as it rotates it develops the great force we know as gravity.

Now gravity is a power, a wavelength, and has adhesion. It is able to change its polarity or rotatory action. The ancients knew this and utilized the energy within gravity to create their vast monuments, but, at the same time we have what is termed the heat or fire force of the Solar system. This you will find referred to in the New Testament,* when a village refused the Christ admittance and a disciple asked if he might send the force of fire to destroy them. It was a reference to the fact that the wave force of energy and heat, could be manifested within a certain radius of perception.

In some of the older religions we find this making or creating of fire by the wavelength ray of energy, was quite a normal thing, but, like so many of these forces, when the energy is abused the knowledge is withdrawn. This does not mean that the energy or the knowledge of life is not being supplied but it is now in an unconscious state where before it was known in the conscious state. What has this to do with our work, our personal development? Once we become aware that these influences and atmospheres are there for the purpose of the evolving consciousness, we can use them in a direct way.

Perhaps the most familiar way is the use of the longer ray which we know as the manifestation of healing. Those who associate themselves with these radiations or emanations, are able to transform the discordancies of the lesser force by the power of a creative force—that is, to arrest corruption and decay, all forms of disease, and then re-create the energy which is lacking; thus the whole atomic structure is altered through the application of this wave force.

One does not need to be religious to be able to use any of these forces. They can be used at the highest or the lowest level, or at the intermediate one. The ideal is to seek these forces only for the good they can do for the evolving purpose. In the healing ray-forces we know that there is a variety of vibrations, and according to our degree of personality we can tune in to a great range of them. Some can tune in to a very high octave of radiating force, to obtain almost instantaneous results with certain types of discordancies.

This is not a question of praying to an invisible something; in the reconstitution of the health pattern we are witnessing the direct application of ray forces which are able to purify, cleanse and strengthen an energy-lacking body, and once we

* Luke 9, verse 54.

31

begin to see that this healing ray is a pleasant and natural thing, and that we can utilize it as a dual part of our living, we can then further apply it to the restoration of harmony in the physical body, and utilize other rays to extend knowledge into the Karmic history and unfoldment of life. This each of us can put to work. Let me take a simple example.

People seem to desire at some time during their life-time to write a book, to put on paper some record or experience of life, either for self-entertainment of for monetary gain. Others seek wealth or position. In fact, we might say that the key to every radiation is the desire force which emanates through each personality. This puts us in tune or sympathy with the ray-force which will supply that particular need. In some cases it is quite pronounced; in others it is merely a passing interest. But if that interest is intense as a conscious thing, then the ray-force which serves that particular part of the evolving principle will concentrate around the need of the personality or desire force, and feed it.

This is done in meditation—to meditate and receive, not to send forth in this instance—in a state of receptivity. This does not require any of the physical faculties at all, in fact, very often the withdrawal of some of the physical faculties has been known to intensify the invisible power. This we all see in art and music where those who have lost the physical faculties have intensified their invisible creativeness to the extent that they have left their mark upon the whole world, and history will record their achievements. So this is not limited to a question of physical force. These rays and forces are the constant means by which the power-house of the Universe is trying to stimulate the awakening mind forces which we should look for and use as a means of intensifying our living. By this intensification we build into one life many lives. By self-work, recognition and the science of matter and evolution, we quicken the life force in its activation. Many would like to be lazy and let life go by in a state of inertness, hoping that something would turn up one day in a wished-for form. There is no dynamo, no energy being received or created, and naturally a state of decomposition

32

sets in very early within that life. But if we can intensify this life pattern, we quicken not only our evolution, but we speed up the whole of the life-force which surrounds us. One person entering upon the esoteric pathway of inward and outward development is really stimulating the atmosphere of everyone near him, although in an invisible way, and by directing these vitalities, energies and impulses into his environment he is quickening the home, the factory, the workshop, the office and, in fact, the whole world around him. People like this are obvious by their intensity of living; they are alive, keen, they look as if they are 'there' and they are constant. In fact they stand out amongst others, for those who know nothing of their way of thinking often say, "These people are different; they are living—they are intense." It is an intensification within the auric pattern which makes them different, which shows there is an attraction of energies and forces, intensifying the consciousness, which in turn quickens the atmosphere of people's perceptions. The self-work of one on the Path unconsciously quickens the Path of many.

We are talking of space as if it were just next door to us—which it is. Space is the vast workshop of the Cosmos, the influencing sea, a great variety of power and influence kept in motion by the Hierarchy, who have in their charge these different rays and radiations which they send forth into the pattern of every race, of other Star forces and revolving Planets. Each one of us must become deeply aware of these great seas and pools of energy, and use them carefully, for we can do harm, in the sense that where a life force has been intensified and quickened it becomes in itself a radiation and an atmosphere. Where before we could lose our temper and it did not matter very much, now it does matter. Where before we could tell the tale and enjoy social gossip, criticize and judge, now we must not. Before our casual thinking was not very powerful, awakened or quickened and it probably did not get very far; when we are intensified in this power force, however, we immediately become a means by which we intensify that which we radiate, at whatever level.

33

That is why we can approach some people who are attuned to or have affinity with certain healing rays or regenerating forces, and very quickly, the whole atmosphere covering the environment of the person needing help, has been changed or altered by the magnetic healing regenerative force set in motion.

But that person so attuned must now be very careful not to hate, nor to live in the emotional, nor let loose in the seas of emotion forces which are negative. It is very necessary now to be aware that these radiations will intensify the negative aspects as well as the positive.

If we seek the intensification and quickening of the evolution of the consciousness and the forces of the life waves, we must discipline the lower faculties and not allow them to run wild.

Often people say they would like to be healers and raise humanity but one knows perfectly well that full powers could never be given to them until they had reached a certain stage of consistency, because it would be dangerous to let them have a power force over and beyond their sense of balance.

Mankind must go forward; we cannot merely stand still in the stream of evolution, for the quickening of the senses, and of the Spirit, and the attuning of ourselves into these great seas of power, knowledge and growth must be accompanied by a Spiritual responsibility, that if we ask for the utilizing of these great forces of the Universe, we shall use them unselfishly, with kindness and discipline.

We all would like to have the power to banish pain, suffering, sickness, illness, injustice, misery and want, but behind these, other things are involved. Just the banishing of them would not solve anything, because if we are in tune with the lesser faculties of these ray-forces we are apt to be creating the very health conditions which we are seeking to dispel.

It is not sufficient to remove pain or a state of want, because unless the responsibility is raised in response towards the new state, people are much safer in that state of want. It is not for us to go in with all our power and prayer and think we are the saviours of mankind, because if we do we are doing a dangerous thing. We are stepping outside the path of wisdom and this needs meditation, non-interference, non-attachment, non-identity. For as soon as we identify ourselves with any emotional outpouring, we immediately trigger off the intensification of that atmosphere.

It is very difficult to withdraw, in order to serve life, but that is what it means. It means a little less human interference, a little more realizing of the Spiritual Cosmic Force which each one of us represents. The limitations are merely the limitations of the brain. The brain is an extension of the mind, and in that extension it is able to manifest according to its sense of responsibility. Increase the sense of responsibility, and the power forces are automatically stepped up likewise. So it is not a matter of praying for this or that. It is by self-work that we equip ourselves to utilize these forces, for they utilize us in the quickening of the evolving principle.

Evolution of the individual is the means of the evolving of the mass; the bringing together of the personal consciousness of the individual urge and awareness deepens and enriches the awareness of a whole society, yet that society is unaware of the influences, atmosphere and enlightenment flowing into it. Thus we have so-called affinities, some in medicine and science, others in physics in different forms, and others in the field of nature, and right through the whole field of affinities—to water, fire and air, etc. And whatever our service is, or where we are directed, we find these forces and rays gathered around us. They enter into the chakras, into the aura and by intensifying the magnetic field that energy, that flow, will pass through our life-force into the life-force of others. This then means, that each seeker on the Path becomes a source of food, a means of energy, of new thinking, of new creativeness, releasing the dormant past into an active future.

Realize that the whole family is involved, by the quickening principle of the life-force being intensified in yourself. Realize that we are living in a tremendous power-house, not only one house but many, many power-houses, and each part, each wave or radiation of that particular power force is serving some different evolving principle. Identify yourself with that principle and that power force and radiation will encompass you and feed you with an intensification of knowledge—known and unknown—protection, guidance, information, stimulation. It is not what we learn in college or school that feeds a life, it is what we acquire from the invisible, the unknown, the unconscious level. Look deeply into what you want. Question the flow of your life. How would you like it to end? Or would not like it to end? What would you really like to do? Centralize yourself. And once you have centralized, keep it constant, and by keeping it constant these forces and powers will be directed to you, and your desire, your need, your hunger, your life-force begins to be fed and sustained from these great waves of thinking energies.

There is no limit to the Universe. There is no limit to what we can achieve, if we like to attune ourselves to the energy flows. These are ours when we decide to believe in them, for they are there, and they are free for us to use and set free in the society of our home or wherever we serve others.

MEDITATION

So let us reach into a new depth, a deeper meaning, into that which is uncharted, the revelation of our capacity, that we may be fed, inspired, and given that participation which each of us needs to fulfil the life principle of our coming.

PART TWO

The Many Kingdoms of the Solar Planes

CHAPTER FOUR

Chemical—Mineral—Body

In all forms of esoteric enlightenment the seeker must progress through the Solar planes, for these are the basic patterns from which the Earth body as such, is created. We are inclined to think of the human body as the beginning and the end, whereas actually we have two bodies on the first and second dimensions.

The human ego uses the earth body as a means of expression and living. The earth body is a composite, a collection, of all the various Planetary systems; and these systems of the Solar planes are all representative of certain forces which maintain and serve the laws of balance and harmony. There are great Beings who live within these Solar planes who are manifestors of the nature forces.

We are inclined to take the ordered Universe very much for granted. We look upon it as a familiar day-to-day event which causes us no wonder. We do not even suspect the intense organization which supports all Planetary life, or know that each form has its own food, seed, origin, purpose and maintenance.

We are dealing now with the mineral world which is governed by Mercury—The Planet of the internal chemistry—also of the astral forces which interpose themselves upon the physical body, so that we have really two levels of chemistry operating on the first-dimensional vehicle at the same time. Thus, we are twofold—an earth body able to manifest and maintain itself within the human body (ego)—by the beat of the heart, the digestion, the circulation, and the anatomical services by which the earth body renders service to the human body—giving us an insight into the evolutionary resources upon which the earth body can, and does, draw. Therefore, there are certain chemical relationships between the Solar influences and the Soul and body forces, which have to be controlled and maintained. Side by side we have two main activators of these. There is an intellectual chemistry working against the effect of superstitious chemistry. We are all aware how this can cause people to become ill or die, and has even affected certain nations to their downfall; demonology and witchcraft, like the witch doctor, belong to the dark ages. There is a superstitious chemistry which we know as the power of suggestion—that what we suggest can change the chemical lines which interweave themselves into the human body and can dramatically interfere with its normal composition and cause temporary or permanent damage—these fears have their source deep down in earth-body memory and, in the ignorant, are easily roused.

We should know of these things because many of them are sub-astral forces which have definite influences—some of which are beneficial. And when we apply them to an intellectual pattern we find that they are not things to fear, for they are the utilization and bringing forth of the life force, to be raised in dimensional activity.

We do not need to stretch the imagination very far to enjoy what we call earth-body relationship. The warmth of the Sun on the body, and the smell of the good soil, the perfume of the trees and leaves, the aroma, the atmosphere, the climate of the Earth itself, the great forces which are released in the surge of Spring, and the chemical forces which operate and nourish the states of what we know as life and fertility, these things are near to us, about us, because they are a part of the natural motherhood—that is, the Earth Mother.

On the one hand we have a Heavenly Father and on the other an Earthly Mother, and each has a tremendous and important part to play in the dual purpose of the unfolding Soul; once we can see that the chemistry is a medium by which one life is projected into another, that the Soul is able to direct these chemical structures, provided it is given opportunities towards definite aims—it helps us to understand spiritual therapies more easily.

The Soul is able, through its human ego, to master the chemical factors, and with the help of Spirit to overcome them in their battle for mastery over the body forces.

Now in sickness we know there is usually a conflict between the earth body and the human body. It seems at times as if there is a distinct opposing relationship between the two, and when this happens a disharmony exists on the astral plane itself. This is not easy to understand at first, but we will simplify it. Some people, for various reasons, hate or resent their earth bodies, and they punish and despise them and use them as a scourge for their Souls, or as a whipping post on which they can lash their consciences, trying to find some form of atonement.

It is more in evidence than we know. We are all liable to take it out of our bodies when we cannot get our own way. We so exhaust the Solar energies and influences within the earth body that it is incapable of efficiently carrying on its natural systems. Thus we have human wilfulness interfering with the balanced energies of the earth body. Here we become aware that emotional balance has a very definite bearing on energy and health, and requires a high degree of responsibility to ensure stamina and endurance.

It is a severe test this emotional interweaving of the chemistry into the mineral world, which mankind, and the Soul too, must face. The Solar body is chemical, composed of mineral and light waves, and these natural resources mingle with the light chemistry—truly the meeting place of Earth, Sun and Heaven.

In the therapeutic field we are aware that the minerals are forces to be reckoned with, for any deficiencies within them affect the overall chemistry, often requiring considerable insight and therapeutic knowledge to correct, so hidden have they become. To harmonize this chemical world is the first law of balance and natural healing.

41

We can do a great deal of this ourselves. We can damage our bodies, or heal them; we can rightly use them or abuse them. The question is how to establish this natural harmony and we find this can best be achieved through right breathing. The breath, the chemistry and the balance of flow between the mineral and the chemical worlds is through the air, through the breath of life.

We find reference to this tremendous transmuting force in the Bible where breath is breathed into life, for life is breath. But in the occult sense it is known as the divine Messenger, the Unifier by which all the lesser or base elements are unified and refined. In illness, we are all the time refining these baser elements, the bad chemistry we have made, trying to eliminate the cross-currents, drawing the vitality back into the earth body, for it is supported by vitality radiating from the Solar forces, in the air we breathe.

Here we begin to see and recognize the wonderful partner-ship which is taking place in the lower planes, where, by right use and understanding, we can remove the causes of discord. Therefore we should know that these natural vitalities and life forces—some of which are quite primitive—are an essential part of our make-up. They are silent forces, sometimes in con-flict or resistance within the earth body, affecting human re-lationships. Most people when they quarrel or are bad tempered are not really bad tempered in the sense of their ordinary character or nature. It is usually a conflict in the mineral or chemical world which becomes at variance within themselves.

The Alchemists referred to this as gall, spleen or liver con-ditions, instead of spite and bad temper, in which the vitality at variance would cause a person to have a sharp tongue, to tell lies, affect their reasoning, carrying them along on a flood of cross-currents; such a person would be living—or expressing— the imbalance of their chemical world. In the many diseases which affect the air, the mineral and chemical worlds, we find there are certain astral associations. If we have abused at any time, or in another life, any of the natural forces of the Solar planes, we have to regain confidence in their use; we have seen

42

certain discordancies which a person has lived through which have been in the form of a transmutation, where they have re-aligned or re-set their lines of force through that particular illness.

It is not necessary—nor should it be so—that we go into the drastic forms of sickness or illness in order that these recoveries of the natural lines or forces should be re-established; this should be done by the application of a higher force, but the average evolutionary necessity is at the disease level, so that compulsory cleansing is unfortunately necessary.

We look at these things with a new vision and insight, re-alizing that illness is not what we thought it to be. This is really a new impression, a new discovery and, rightly under-stood, it will remove conflict. Any chemist will tell you that conflict is a first reaction in the field of chemistry. Very use-ful! but at the same time it can be a dangerous thing, some-times it emerges harmoniously, at other times it explodes violently.

These reactions are not confined to the minerals of the Earth alone, but are of the air also, for in the air and atmosphere exist the finer ether essences of the chemical world, and their gases have the ability to change and convert chemical sub-stances.

I have seen such a conversion occur where the breath of a person was used effectively to change the chemistry effects in another person's body. In many of the Yoga practices breath and healing were used together—in some cases they still are. A gauze or silk handkerchief is held over the afflicted part and is breathed on and through, until at last the breath has cleansed that part of the body and replenished the cells; drastic changes have been known to occur in this way. To my mind it is hard work, and to those who do not understand, it can be disquieting to see breath being used directly on to an afflicted body. I mention this in passing as a matter of interest, to show that the healing forces of air and breath have a definite creative energy, and can refine chemical substances and structures. Now we begin to realize that the Solar Plane contains not only heat

43

and the natural radiations of the colour spectrum but many types of essential gases which are formed through Sunlight itself. Thus the Sun is our Solar power-house, and an absence from it for any length of time causes a breakdown in the vitamins or chemical composition of the body, and if the lack is prolonged the whole chemical system will break down. On the other hand, if it is over-exposed it can over-precipitate the chemistry lines and have a detrimental effect. But in the West it is the lack, rather than over-supply, that causes deficiencies.

When we study the influence of Mercury and its Astrological signs, we find that the skin, being an extension of the lungs, is the first to be affected by Solar radiations, chemical or mineral decomposition. This shows itself first in skin ailments or impurities, caused by the body trying to resist or throw out the chemical compositions which are poisonous to it, through the lungs and out through the skin. This inner cleansing through eruptions on the outer form has been actually recognized as a Soul force in action, and in the early days the different forms of skin disease, such as leprosy and so on, were usually associated with a spiritual or astral cause. This is to a certain extent true.

In all forms of psychological and emotional troubles, those healers with a spiritual background have a better effect among patients than those who are merely interested in the anatomical system. Some nuns and priests have had wonderful cures through being able to influence the astral side of the afflicted person, especially when influenced by atmospheres such as at Lourdes. This means that there are other forms of chemistry which are able to refine the atom structures, such as a higher power of thinking, being and breathing which we exert in prayer.

In Yoga, as in most of the deeper and older religions, breathing is taught as part of the cleansing of the body and Soul, releasing the essence of Prana Spirit. Very few of us do any deep breathing. We do not realize that we are dealing with very powerful human and spiritual forces which balance, harmonize, cleanse, restore and maintain us. It is a good thing for everybody to take deep breathing exercises first thing in the morning, especially if they are lying flat in bed warmly tucked up instead of standing at an open window doing their best to catch a chill! This cleansing of the lungs from the poisons of the night, and starting the day with clean oxygen in the blood, was originally part of the esoteric teaching—the cleansing at dawn and rising of the Sun—and was a natural part of the student's work, from an early age, as health training. In our modern times we can still do this and restore a large amount of natural energy which would not normally be available. It is the morning rays at sunrise in conjunction with the healing breath which can do us the most good.

As we go a little further in knowledge we find definite chemistry and definite minerals we can utilize—the Heavenly Father over the Earthly Mother. Many old forms of therapy utilized this transmutation, where the forces from the evolved, refined, higher Solar planes could be brought to bear on the lower in a form of healing, and which was very widely practised in ceremonies of Sun worship. The Sun worshippers, as a whole, were very healthy people, who achieved tremendous vitality and creativeness. Their sensitivity to the Solar planes was such that they could replenish their earth body energies and so produce healthy human bodies; they sought knowledge and efficiency to transmute the lower into the higher, via worship and Sunlight and seeking the aid of Spiritual Sun Beings.

I once saw this done. It was a very short ceremony, which impressed me a great deal at the time. It took place in an open field, and the sick person who had a running ulcer, was laid across a boulder which was at a certain level, with the twelve signs of the Zodiac surrounding it, and as the Sun passed at a particular angle across the sore it dried and healed. We know that the Solar forces were used in the Sun temples for direct nature cure, and in exposing ourselves to the Sun we are not only exposing the earth body, and human body, we are drawing in through the astral more refined chemistry and mineral supplies. So the body should become purer and cleaner by exposure to the natural elements.

Here is the point where self-work comes in, that is, the thought-chemistry of life, a pattern which is amenable to any change we like to impose upon it. To return to this question of the ego being able to master its full assignment of life—that is, for the Soul to be able to live to the full, time assigned for its residence here, to be able to manifest and hold in balance these forces to which it has been exposed. The Bible refers to this as "Physician, heal thyself". We can look at it in aother way and call it self-healing, by the recognition of the natural forces brought under control.

As we have said, we can destroy the body or we can raise it up. Thought-life itself is the key to the chemistry factor of the earth body—that is, we can create finer chemicals or we can fashion lower ones, for as we think, so does our chemistry work. We can create poisons, toxins, excessive waste, or we can produce lighter variations of useful chemical particles, and working with the higher atom, light structures instead of heavy ones.

By living a life of resentment, conflict, dissatisfaction, criticism, vanity, pride, jealousy, and so on, we produce very low chemical atoms and the results of these can be seen in the state and condition of the body. If there is a weakness existing in the body we cause that to become active through feeding it from lower levels.

We shall deal with this in density and weight, because some people can produce what we call light bodies and others produce heavy bodies. This is not a question of weight on the scales, it is an ethereal effect, and the whole body seems to glow with a factor of light radiation. Some people work, talk, think and live entirely on the light side of the atom form, while others live on the heavy side and seem miserable, downcast, ever complaining and always in a state of weight, over-burdened and usually heavy laden. This is the thought-life in action, so we see that, apart from the knowledge of our basic chemistries, we can begin to refine it by a higher and different line of thought. Even by studying these lectures at this stage, we are actually commencing the refining. We are beginning to concentrate on the lighter atom, instead of the heavy, gravitational atom which we are prone to manufacture.

'Cleanliness is next to Godliness' and I think that a person with a light body is near that culmination. There is something light and joyous and gentle about them. So transparent are the particles of their human bodies that one can almost see through some of them, and the refining discipline and balance of the earth body is such that the Soul is able to manifest to far higher degree than it could do, if it had to fight its way through a dense body, through a difficult, eruptive chemistry.

I hope I have been able to stimulate you into knowing, being more aware of these invisible structures which surround us. They are created as a part of the earth-plane body, and we are Planetary Beings; we shall occupy Planets other than this, and in each we shall use the method of chemistry and the minerals of which that Planet is principally made. As we pass through these various systems on our Planetary journey through Stars into outer space and the denser worlds, and back from the denser worlds into the lighter worlds, we shall take with us our history, and above all our experience, and if we can make more application and utilization of the various Planetary and Solar influences we shall return useful people instead of almost as ignorant as when we started out. So you see there is much to be done on this worldly journey. There are Planetary Beings with whom we are in partnership and who are training us to participate in their work, so that in turn we can effectively operate within these fields or zones, in further assignments or work, in different lives.

So anything we can do by removing friction, by feeding and entering into a new relationship with our body, we should do. Talk to it, treat it as a friend, but it needs discipline just as an animal needs discipline— because it is animal. It needs kindness and firmness and as an animal will run away or do too much, it needs the touch of a master, and the human body is master of the earth body. As we step up from the human body to the astral body and finally to the Spirit, we see that these levels of energy flow one into the other and are each a part of the Creative Force. By entering into a state of knowing and discipline we shall become on good terms with the Solar influences, and our health pattern will become much more reliable; our work for the future is going to be decided by our interest and application and self-work here.

MEDITATION

Now we will attune to this idea. We are participating in the form of an earth body and a human body—a Heavenly Father and Nature Mother. We form the trinity between these two parents, composed of all the Planetary qualities and these are expressing themselves in the chemistry, the minerals, and in the breath. By right living we can utilize these forces to a far more effective, beneficial and useful degree. Meditate on this quietly and earnestly.

CHAPTER FIVE

Air—Breath—Life

Here we are dealing with the workshop of the elements, particularly the therapeutic necessity of understanding our human relationship to the natural elements of the earth, also to bring in the deeper implications of why these creations exist at all. When we use such a broad universal subject as Air and unify it with Breath and Life, we are really trying to embrace in words the three greatest Creative Forces.

Breath, or air, is also within the sign of Mercury, and as well as the lungs it controls all the factors of continuity in our earthly body. Air is able to renew and replace itself very quickly; it can be re-energized from outer space or from local or Planetary life. Oxygen and hydrogen are the two gases which together sustain life. These form a combined fluid on which we are able to draw and which we consume in great quantities; yet the reservoir is never exhausted, for it is a permanent part of the perpetual energy resources of the Cosmic Universe. In looking further we see that air is the basis of combustion, making possible the elements of fire; so air and fire become twins which live and work together as partners, for wherever we find air we find fire, and where there is fire there must be air, for fire cannot exist without its twin and both rely upon each other to perform their cleansing and renewal. Thus, we see that the flame purifies with air and has an influence which affects everything it touches; it is part of the natural process by which all matter and substance is cleansed and restored, and this continual purification takes place throughout the entire life cycle from the moment of birth till the time of passing.

We are enshrouded and embodied in a great sea of cleansing and of nourishment which we use very freely, usually taking it for granted—seldom do we think of the Science of GOD which can maintain such a reservoir of nourishment and perpetual food; a form of conversion by evolution.

To think of air as food may be to some rather a new way of looking at part of our diet, but of all the elements, air, or the breath of life, is the essential; the others are auxiliary to our need, but air is the first condition of consciousness. So we find that breath and consciousness are the unifying forces of the evolving life principle. If we remove air, the life principle as we know it could not work, neither could consciousness express itself in the density of matter. The interesting thing about this force is that it is bi-dimensional, for a more rarified air exists on many higher planes. The Heavens themselves depend on HIS Holy Breath—the oceans of air carry the great Solar perfumes of the Stellar masses, and as we pass from one layer, or plane, to another we are served by these rarified systems. Each Star represents a system and in the Star or earth body is a corresponding process; each process forms a function which Astrologers term the ruling sign of that function or organ. Thus, the lungs and skin are ruled by Mercury and represent the first Planetary system of birth. In our next cycle we shall retain the lungs, the respiratory organs, but we dispense with the digestive organs. Some of you, no doubt, will be quite pleased to hear of this as an understanding sign from Heaven—that there will be no necessity for cooking and washing-up, or any of the other time-consuming activities in the partaking of food as we know it! If we look clearly at the amount of food we eat and the amount of air we consume, we find that the air is far greater in quantity and quality than the food we absorb from Planetary plant life. For this reason the Greeks and other ancients built temples, not only in adoration to the Sun, the Moon and the Stars, but to the Spirits of the wind. And the Greeks portrayed these by the pillars on the top of their hills in eight slender columns. The symbol of the air is eight, and these slender columns with the dome of the Heavens over them were where the Spirits of the wind could rest in their travelling. I like the idea! To me it is delightful! It sounds something very gentle, kindly and understanding. These eight-column temples on the hills have often been misconstrued as for fire-worship, but their original meaning was as temples to the Spirits of wind. "He took the wind where it listeth, and brought drought and rain and frost and heat, and dispensed them to the children of the Earth according to their needs."

Air contains the Spirit of life, the state of Being we know as consciousness. Without it our brains could not work, we should not be able to think or live as we do. It is difficult enough even to visualize life with stagnant water, let alone stagnant air or in a vacuum; air is movement and movement feeds evolution, thus air and its flow carries the Solar warmth, and the sequences of the seasons is tied to the Spirit or the Breath of life. When we think of time and seasons as sequences or measures we must also visualize air pressures, and those great oceans of air currents which control the Planetary systems we know as Spring, Summer, Autumn and Winter, for these respond to the great Celestial Solar time rhythm and are the very heart beat of the Heavens. For this reason we should understand the Celestial aspect of air. This is what the Bible tries to depict in Genesis —that GOD Breathed and life took place. This is referred to by esoterics as "the Divine Ignition" where the forces of life are able to join up with the forces of intelligence, so that intelligence, thought, reason and air are all a part of this Divine Ignition, whereby mankind and all the elements are fired into consciousness and Being. We only need a very slight drop in the oxygen capacity for the mind to go to sleep. The brain can only operate for 15 minutes without oxygen. After that it is so badly damaged that it cannot operate any more. The whole cell tissue of the body depends upon a continual Celestial oxygen to maintain the Spirit within life as we know it here. So we can see then that the Breath of Life is over and above and throughout. It is a part of the silent yet moving invisible picture which not only sustains creation

51

as it has been made, but makes possible further creation in that it is the great transmitter. It is the means by which the whole Universe communicates, by means of sound, perfume and the subtle gases; it is not only the transmitter of knowledge, but it is also something even more valuable in that it is a great vibrational medium to which matter and density responds. We are used to the magnetic ether vibrations through which man is able to transmit impulses from one continent to another. We are only now beginning to understand that air waves and heat waves have their own supersonic effect, and are thus able to produce actual climatic conditions by the rhythm of their motion. Now these tremendous air forces which soar above our Planet are quite different from those we know at the surface level. These winds blow at four-hundred, five-hundred, even thousands of miles an hour, and we must admit that this tremendous movement which cleans and renews our climate and protects the lower air streams from radiations, is a Celestial Workshop indeed. As these forces produce, by their own friction and movement, magnetism and electricity, so do they bind and feed the lower atmospheres of air upon which all human and Planetary life depends. So in outer space and even on the fringe of space we find the Spirit of air working continuously, season by season, producing nourishment and maintaining balance and order.

Now the interesting thing about the ancient temples of the Spirits of the air is that all religious teachings were founded in oral explanations, and if we care to study the basic beginnings of the various religions we find that they are all air-taught—that is, they were verbally taught in the open air. Christianity is a typical example of the teaching of the Word in the open—where the desert and the Sun, the rocks, the lakes, streams and the sand were the natural setting, the natural surrounding elements in which the Word was given forth.

In Buddhism we find the same thing true—truth was for the open, it was not for the closed-in, the frustrated, shuttered, restricted and imprisoned. So when we really begin to discover the true esoteric basis of the different forms of religion we find that as soon as it becomes imprisoned, whether in buildings, in books or accessories, we lose something very important to its freedom. We imprison the word, but it should not be restricted, it should remain free and visionary. This is why our student courses are dependant on the spoken—never the written—word.

The Word of Truth or Breath of Life, should still flow in this method of personal transmission and teaching, through natural visionary sources. Most of you, I expect, at some time or another have felt so hemmed in and congested that you longed to stand on a hill top with the head bare to let the wind blow through your hair. Like a Celestial cleansing, it purifies, strengthens and restores your sense of freedom.

This is really the symbol of air, its tremendous freedom and its continual motion, its ability to transmit, its restlessness; soothing, yet stimulating at the same time.

The Soul and the Spirit respond more quickly and beneficially when they are in a true element which belongs to natural surroundings—that is, in openness and movement.

There are people who have what we term a closed nature—they like everything tightly sealed, locked, tied and hidden. They do not like too much fresh air. The air is not their medium. Fire, perhaps, but not air. So they draw the curtains, shut everything up tightly, often feeling insecure if they are exposed too much to open spaces. They have not a natural sympathy with the poetry of freedom. This is something in the nature and character that needs more open development.

We all have some special affinity with the elements in that they are great cleansers; some find in water a sense of freedom and buoyancy and invigoration. Yet others are distrustful or fearful of the ocean and find it restrictive. These fears of the elements show that those who have them have yet to become on good terms with the creative forces; some part of their nature and character has still to experiment and new discoveries are to be made that will increase their knowledge and understanding.

It has been said that every true prophet and seer is eventually able to manifest within all the elements. We find this in early Christian teaching where the control of water, air, and of fire, gravity and abundance were all a part of the open-visionary force used by the prophets and the other ancient teachers. It was because of this close and near association with the natural forces of the Creative Universe that they were able to demonstrate what some call miracles; in demonstrating their power of affinity and association of common union, they were able to bring into usefulness and purpose the mind force which these forces represent. We must consider each element as a great God-Being. We must think of our Planet as a great Planetary Being; think of atoms, electricity and light as infinite power resources working within these Planetary 'seas of energy', able to penetrate, control, balance and harmonize all these forces for beneficial use.

Here we must remember that, although we are accustomed to the main elements of our own Planet, these elements are general to all the systems, they are not only contained in our small world in space. There are Celestial powers, Celestial workshops in the great Cosmic oceans of outer space, within other Planets which partake of the Universal Life Force which radiates to the lesser Planets. Strangely enough the scientists have just stumbled on to this, though it was known as metaphysical truth many, many centuries ago—that the force and substance of life comes from outer planets of space. Science has also discovered that, at certain periods, there is a tremendous surge of energy that seems to come in one direction at certain cycles or periods, and there is no scale by which it can be measured, judged or weighed. It makes every known form of power or energy as we know it, look small and insignificant, an awe-inspiring discovery among those who are studying Cosmology and Astronomy; the mightiness, the magnitude of these flow atoms which can form and perpetuate through space this unity of purpose and control.

Here we see that Spiritual science is keeping pace with third-dimensional science, that is, there is an opening up of what was once considered myth or legend, and these things, which were thought to be of dubious origin and which were derided, now become acceptable by scientific finding.

So the human scientist is becoming more in tune with the spiritual and science has not out-dated GOD—it is not disproving Divine origin, it is substantiating it. I do not like to think that the bishops of tomorrow must be the scientists of today!—but perhaps that may be the way in which it must take its course.

As seekers on this Path, having an interest mainly in the therapeutic side of these great forces within the body, we can visualize its tremendous importance here, as well as in the function and cycles in the worlds which are still in the process of being made—worlds which one day you and I will occupy, and we shall look back on this short journey of earth-restricted discipline as a very insignificant and minute experience in the great supreme order of experiences. But nevertheless, at this time, while we are engulfed in it, it will absorb and dominate our very thinking life. We can raise these visionary scenes, however, and see the elements in the workshop of the Almighty, working not only for the benefit of the human race as we know it now, but forming Systems and Stars and Planets far lighter and far greater than this or anything we can conceive. Then, by the very vision of this, we shall help to make possible the communication between them. Only as we become aware can we be efficiently taught and trained. If a person has absolutely no knowledge or awareness, or they live in a vacuum of unawareness, it is essential to form and build a basic foundation, a basic vision, a simple pattern of knowledge which they can use as a creative tool; until this is done it is almost impossible to raise them from their mechanical life and their shut-in existence.

So those on the Path have to be aware, as Ouspensky has already said, not only of the mechanical motion in response to the evolving Universe, but also see ourselves as Spiritual scientists capable of receiving communications from a higher level, from a deeper source and wider perspective.

We are beginning to suspect, and I think it is true, that the consciousness of the Soul is life, and the more we can extend this life and consciousness the quicker we shall realize the great hidden Celestial Force contained in the human society. The key to this is, as the old esoterics have always maintained, to release man from self; release him into this wonderful Universe, and set in motion the ultimate result.

In studying these elements, the servants of the Cosmos, we try to release their consciousness into our natural surroundings. So it is not only air we breathe into our lungs but the knowledge that the air can give us. The ancients used to refer to this as Prana, which feeds the body cell by cell, and so reconstructs its life force as to be able to bring news and information to the cell structure, instructing it in the forming of a new body.

We now hear another word, D.N.A.*—which is thought to be the carrier of the genetic code and is thus able to communicate knowledge. We have understood that Prana was the communicator of the invisible forces, so our bodies can change and their chemistry can alter, for the whole of the structure of the body is under continual teaching and transformation. It is being brought up-to-date by immunization from disease, refashioning, reshaping and reforming of new patterns and forces of resistance to disease—all these things depend on new information that we draw through the deep breath of life. Once we understand this we begin to realize that it is indeed Holy, Holy Breath, for it is sustaining us at many levels, most into our lungs or extracts of third-dimensional needs.

Now to finalize. To what is this applied, and what contribution will it make? This brings us right back to self-study, to self-discipline. If we have the Holy Breath and use it, it is communication from the Gods. It is sustenance to the body, it is freedom to the Soul. Also we must watch it as the communicator, and mind what language we use it for. If we use it rightly then we raise its consciousness, but if we deform it, lower it, depress it, by using it for judgment, criticism, or all the other horrid things of which the mind of Adam and Eve is capable, then we poison the great Spirit of air and impede its evolution.

* Deoxyribonucleic acid.

We must also see to it that neither by word nor thought shall we pass on a message of cruelty and selfishness, but that only the Divine message shall go from us. We shall not pass on to the human race further misery, further suffering, but shall pass on the Word of fulfilment, inspiration, encouragement, truth and freedom. This is a part of your self-work to visualize this great Holy Breath, this great element of the Universe, feeding your body, being utilized by your mind, your intelligence and your thought. By communicating the very Breath of Life, we shall know we are living in the Spirit of the Creator.

MEDITATION

With this thought in mind let us sit in meditation for a few moments and realize that the Spirit of the Comforter will give the Breath of Life, and the seekers of Life are those who value the beauty of these elemental forces which sustain us, and are a living part of ourselves. May we do our part in self-work to release them into their full creative capacity, that our lives be as silver chains to continue in thought and capacity long after we have left our present scene.

CHAPTER SIX

Water—Gases—Fluids

Truly to understand the importance of the Solar planes to the Earth Life, we must first of all appreciate that life on Earth is a projection of the Solar planes themselves. The Earth with its lower cycle is dependent entirely upon the Solar cycle for its orderliness and its seasons, and for all its natural forms of sentient life as we know them. In other words, we are only lodgers in the sense of living on an outer Planet, that depends entirely on another Planet for its livelihood.

And so, from outer space, from the parent to the small system, as we are, is radiated a force, controlling the influences and the power energies which we know as Earth life. There is no Earth life in itself, except that which is produced and maintained from the Solar planes themselves.

Thus we begin to see that we are in a state of receptivity, very much a nursery Planet, evolving at a very low rate in the orbit of evolution. We are only on the fringe; we are in the cradle of evolution, and we are still experiencing the primitive force of outer space. Naturally, when we have a Planet which is in a sub-controlled state, such as ours, we are necessarily controlled and influenced by the cycles and the phenomena or activities of the other Planets, and these supply us with our different resources. The Sun plays upon and activates the waters of Earth, and from these it is able to produce a very rich and varied harvest, dependent on the length of light, and the various energies and rays which form the belt of sun light as we know it. These waters are then set in motion and flow, condense, and distribute themselves over the earth's surface, taking with them the Solar rays, and energies, which have been absorbed by the water and are then deposited directly into the soil. So Solar energies are really foods in a transient state which are being projected into the various materials of earth and form a life basis from which fertility can grow.

So fertility stems entirely from the Solar soil. There is no fertility within the earth except that which is provided from the Solar planes themselves. As we go further we shall begin to see more and more that we are actually living from the Sun itself, and it is from the Sun planet—the parent Planet of our Solar system—that we are multiplying, producing, thinking and creating. Without these constant energy resources interplaying into the atmosphere of the earth, there would only be darkness and non-fertility.

We see now that all the waters of life are formed into what we call the gaseous fluids. The water itself is only oxygen and hydrogen, and these two gases mixed together can coagulate into a solid densified form. So solidification, that is, fluid in density, is really a different form of Solar material which acts under certain vibratory influences to merge together to become substance or matter as we know it.

There again we must see the mountains as they react to the sky as catchment areas which collect the harvest of the clouds, and in the gleaning of this harvest bring it down to earth and feed it through the great gorges of the rivers and lakes and seas, and multiply it through the chemicals of the earth until it comes to the plains as living food.

The mountains may not seem to be working very hard, but they are part of the irrigating and fertilizing system of the Planet, the vast reserve energies from the solar planes. If there were no mountains we should not have controlled water resources, held in reserve by glaciers, snow and ice. Low temperature regions storing fuel radiated from hot temperature zones.

That there is a Plan behind the plan is the very fact that makes possible, for example, the tremendous systems of hydro-electricity. The next time you are standing near a waterfall and see the water pouring forth, look at it and realize that you are actually witnessing a Solar dynamo of the Sun forces at work; Solar energy flowing on earth which originated from far away in outer space. You are witnessing in that simple cascading pattern the presence of the great orderliness of the outer and inner Planetary systems.

These control patterns make possible what we call the density of fluids, the density of gases, the density of earth, and the inter-changing of life.

So we see that the Solar forces are also linked to the land masses, each one keyed into this heart of creativeness. The mountains have always been considered holy places, in their silence and immensity and loneliness, and in this the Ancients were quite right. They are often inhabited by Solar Beings.

To understand 'Being' I want you to realize that primitive thought was not far wrong. In early times they would seek signs from the Gods who offered guidance in their own way, and would even ask permission to plant and sow or undertake any enterprise, so that they should be blessed by the Gods.

Now this is quite interesting because we know that each Master of the Solar rays also has an equivalent counterpart on Earth. This may seem rather strange but communication must be two-way, a communicator and a receiver, a transmitter and one who receives what is transmitted. And many holy mountains, especially in the Himalayas and other such remote places were, and are the homes of the Solar Teachers, the Solar Masters, who make possible the receptive waves entering into the earth, harnessing them and bringing them into a sequence of law and order. This is not a fairy tale or an imaginary thing. We cannot have an orderly Universe without having those who are responsible for its orderliness. We cannot have a highly controlled, progressive, evolutionary state without having great minds, great intelligences, and enormous resources to feed and maintain this great project of life maintenance. We could not live in a series of accidents and collisions, nor could we be left to be playthings of destiny. There must be a project. There must be a purpose; there must be a plan. And it is this idea of an evolutionary plan that the Masters fed, or willed, into man's early ideas of 'GOD'—Gods in the plural, Gods of the Sun, Gods of the Deep, and so on. Every aspect of nature through primitive man's ideas was embodied in a God form.

Now this is not wrong. As we understand more about the Solar reflections—that is the tremendous resources of power and energy transmitted from the Solar to the earth Beings—we find that there is a necessity for these controlling Beings, these 'Solar Gods' if you like, that they should control manifestation in its lower form.

There are those, of course, who profess to have a special interest in some of these Gods and their works, and set up in business for themselves—such as the rainmakers and bringers of fertility and good harvests—they seem to make quite a good thing out of it! Such is superstition. But I want to go one step further and try to put to your minds a mental co-operative idea in which we can visualize that GOD has many sides— lesser Gods, and that there are many Servers along the evolutionary spiral, from the Divine Centre into the far-flung Star centres of the outer Stellar spaces.

We are rather inclined to think of one God as one system. This no doubt simplifies certain forms of thinking but, on the other hand, it complicates them into various religions. We find that the 'God' was plural and only later, in the Jewish faith, was the single God idea brought into being and lesser Gods wiped away. The Egyptians did not believe in this idea, nor did any of the ancient religions. They all knew of these great Masters and Beings who were linking and accepting those more highly evolved, to respond and respect them, to communicate with them, and with them be able to be participate in the future creative pattern of Solar plane evolution.

It is from this area of thinking we have the idea of punishment, that we either co-operated with these Teachers and Masters or, if we did not, we were cursed or dispossessed. That may seem rather odd, but if you study history you will find it is true—the various people who sought to destroy or deny the evolutionary plan of the human race were sooner or later destroyed or removed by evolutionary events.

This also makes sense in another way—in that GOD has many servants and that the Godhead is made up of a tremendous Hierarchy of very highly refined and beautiful Beings who give their entire life service to the evolutionary progress of others.

Now the same thing applies to human beings, because we are, in a way, Gods in training. We are also being conditioned to experience the different levels of these great waves of energy and force at the receiving end, because one day we shall be at the creating source, and we shall then know both sides of the positive and negative flow fields. We also shall become attached to or even be servants of the lesser Gods, for we know that each is apprenticed to some special life service and through this direct experience of living, unfoldment grows. The Solar planes give us our first glimpse of these training activities, where we participate much better with our eyes open than by blindly existing in an orderly Universe without giving credit to these tremendous encompassing Beings, kindly, faithful Intellects, who have the evolutionary progress of the human family in their hands.

Again we can see the Solar plane, the fluids, the waters and the gases, as a sending forth and a withdrawal; when that which is sent forth is exhausted it is drawn back. We find that life is contained in fluid; in fact, our bodies are 95 per cent fluid; our memories are fleeting impressions of density, but real Life Force is of Spirit and belongs to the higher dimension that represents itself temporarily in this lesser watery body.

Thus, Solar energies melt the fluids into vapour, and the purified vapour returns to earth and so the cycle of renewal passes backwards and forwards over the earth's surface, ensuring a constant sweetness and cleanliness which we recognize as Godliness. It seems as if this two-way flow from unclean to clean is the nursery whereby the vital forces are constantly maintained, going back and forth between the sky and the earth, and through the earth into the atmosphere. And so the great dynamo of the Earth Planet and the Solar planes create this vast sea of energy which we know as living life.

What we call the Ocean is really creativeness, manifested by thought, in water. Thought is like fluid, like a gas, and from the gaseous worlds we harness our creations; we have our lubricants and oils, nourishment for plant life and the harvest of the seas, and we enjoy the intermediate state by which fluids temporarily become solids. All this is the important part of man's expression of creativity, in that he uses the fluids of substance and moulds them into the shapes of his mind. We see a vast building, and we realize that this is made of concrete, bricks and cement; but the whole structure was moulded, made from fluid, poured into moulds and allowed to solidify—and there we have our towns and city buildings. Every day we witness this process of fluids and gases passing into partial states of solidification. This we know as density and, therefore, we see our civilization and environment as represented through these moulds which were poured, shaped and formed.

Now the thing to remember is that one dimension overshadows another. To those of the Solar and higher planes, our world is still in a state of gaseous change. To us a concrete wall is quite a barrier to our vibration of matter, but to the Higher Beings it is not a concrete wall, but just a mist or vapour which can therefore be passed through because density does not resist them. They are able to pass through from one zone—or density —to another at will.

Density is but a rate of consciousness. We can pass through the various densities as we rise in consciousness. The lower planes are formed and sustained of partially solidified fluids. Therefore, the 'arisen' can come from the depths of the ocean or through the fastness of concrete and stone. To the freed consciousness that enters it becomes a new vibrating world, and the Soul passes through these vibrations into further stages of reality. This helps us to understand a little more why these higher Beings take to themselves Solar-plane bodies. Now a Solar-plane body is rather different from an earth body. Remember, in another part of our work we dealt with the earth

63

body and the human body, and now we can begin to realize that there is a Solar body, and this is composed of the light atoms which radiate from the Sun. Now, just as energy, food, vitality, electricity, magnetism, hydrogen, oxygen, helium and all the forces which warm our life are actually sent to us from the Solar planes, so, as we in our turn utilize them, these give us a glimpse of the inter-relationship of Planet to Planet, Star to Star, System to System, and the many Suns to the great Sun—a Jacob's Celestial ladder of ascension from dimension to dimension, and how each feeds into the great Evolutionary Principle—a spiral by which we enter into the lighter ethers and into that rarefied state of living, freed from the vibrations, the gases and the fluids that we know here as life. Of such are Solar bodies composed.

Another point we should remember, is that although we think of heat and warmth—there is actually no such thing. The sensation of heat comes from ray energies, and these ray energies are fed into the different oceans of energy through which they pass and are converted by these oceans, or atmospheres, into what we call heat, cold, electricity, magnetism, gamma rays, solar rays, and so on.

This is why it is so cold on the top of a mountain and so warm in the valley when the Sun is giving forth heat. We could argue that, as we get nearer to the Sun we should be hotter on the top of a mountain and cooler in the valley. This is not so, of course, and it illustrates to us that heat as we know it, is not actually passed to us from the Sun, but there are tremendous ray forces which strike our atmosphere and cause molecular and atomic friction, and the light rays passing through the atmosphere agitating the light atoms causes movement and produces the warmth that we feel. Thus the warmth that we know is a Solar radiation sent out as perhaps even cold light, and re-converted by each Planet through its envelope of vapours, fluids and gases, into the products that are needed to sustain its life.

So really even the fluids and gases are the products of light passing through their various forms of change, and we register these

64

as neons, oxygen and hydrogen and all the other various forms of gases. Some we use and some we do not, but invariably the whole of the plant and sea life is in tune with certain ray energies upon which they depend for their very existence. Many of these energies are not yet known to man. We know some, however, and our scientists have now accepted the existence of what we call 'Cosmic rays.' These have been photographed on sensitive films as 'white snow', and they actually pass right through the earth. The Earth itself is a vaporous, semi-gaseous solid, and the Cosmic rays pass through it in the same way as electricity passes along wires as current.

So you see we are nebulous people. We are really gas, walking about in these vapour bodies of ours; they creak often from lack of lubrication and become very worn and tattered, but the body is still only a steamy tank of water, atoms and vaporous fluid life-force, and one day we shall learn how to renew these bodies. Beyond, on the other plane, bodies are cast off, renewed, and re-made instantly. The same thing happens here only we do it more slowly, cell by cell. That is cell-multiplication on a very low cycle, with the result that we are not able, at our state of density, to maintain a more rapid rate of regeneration. Therefore, because we are slower in vibration, our bodies catch up with us! This gives us the idea of age, the tempo of our rate of cell reproduction is so slow that we experience slow disintegration. Imagine calling this 'home'!

We can dehydrate the body by different ways, so we fill it with poisons and saturate it with tea and false comfort! We must see ourselves merely as inhabitants of these zones of fluids and gases, using them as a means of divine irrigation. Blood courses through the veins and water passes through the glands and the various systems and functions of the body, but air and water are our main foods.

Now, here I want to go back to our primitive ideals. These ideals were born of a state of necessity; they were not the product of theological deduction. They were the result of hard and painful experience, and experience is a religion in itself because it is a teacher. I am referring now to the idea of Sun-worship. We are all Sun-worshippers, consciously or unconsciously. We only need a long, hard winter and we are crying out for the Sun. To feel the warmth of the Sun in our bones is not only the warmth of the Solar plane, but the renewing of the vitalities and energies which in the winter solstice, become depleted so that the body in its fatigued state becomes depressed. So Sun food, Sun warmth, Sun light, has a tremendous Spiritual uplift, and it seems to be linked very much to a spiritual sense of well-being, joyousness and promise of Eternal Life. The wonder of Spring strikes us anew every year. It is always new, and it never ages, never grows old; this reaching up or out to the Home, or Homes, from which have come, is inborn in every life.

The Sun rays come as a messenger. Just as we expect and look for letters and news from home, Sunlight is our correspondence. It is our news, it is the means by which we can rebuild these faded, vaporous bodies of ours, to make them a little healthier, stronger and better to live in, because they do get a bit sorry sometimes, and we lose the essence of vitality. Sun-worship was essentially a means of praising the Gods who sent forth this tremendous abundance upon the Earth, and the festivals of most of the old religions, Christian as well, are really linked to the old Sun festivals. We will not go into that here, but as you participate in the great Solar resources, realize the tangible and intangible, recognize your true place in this Solar spiral of evolution to the life principle.

Now the idea of the Sun religions was to participate and enter into a true relationship. I am sure that this is a good way to find the centre of the Spirit, because as we go into the country and see anew the trees, grass and flowers, and the natural life, we seem to get very near to communication—and something happens to us where communication takes place. We go back to beauty and serenity. The Sun-worshippers were not so pagan as we thought!

If we can link the Sun as a servant to the great Divine Ignition, that is the great principle of life and form, we enjoy not only its sense of warmth and Being, but also remember

66

those who are in charge of them. When a shaft of life or Sunlight comes through a wood and dances on the forest floor and the stories of the fairies and gnomes and elves who dance round it comes to mind, it sounds like romance—perhaps it is, but enjoy it!

Now we, with our esoteric knowledge, seeing evolution going through its great chain of experiences and processes, can often stand and watch the great God-Beings participating with us too. If we can view that moment as a little child would see it, and dance with joy in the wet dew, take our shoes off and feel that lovely vibrant fluid, the very dew of the Heavens, welling up between our toes, in that moment, we shall perhaps be nearer to GOD than in the singing of any hymn.

And believe, when there is a rainbow, that you are witnessing the handiwork of the Gods. Stop and admire and give a little prayer, and you will find that you are actually communicating with those Beings and they will intensify the beauty as we recognize it. Sensitivity sees a form of beauty that lack of sensitivity does not even know exists.

A more beautiful world is created and enjoyed once we begin to see the natural mechanics, the natural forces, and those wonderful People who are involved in their maintenance, in the control, in their guiding, in their beautifying, see the colour of a flower as a message from the great Divine Source. Electricity, lightning, the rainbow, the waterfall, the very rain, the mist on the grass and the dew are all part of the great Solar-plane activity, so do not take them for granted!

There is a sense of sadness for those Servers of the Gods when they see human beings trampling ruthlessly across their treasures without a feeling of sensitivity or sharing. It is as if, when you have done a fine job of work, nobody could care less or wants to stop and admire, or even give a word of thanks or encouragement. Lack of appreciation is a fall from grace—and density at its worst.

Thus in moments of stillness when you are communicating with the 'Gods within the Gods', and through them to the Divine Principle of GOD, I want you to see the Solar planes participating with us, in a very intimate, personal, lovely, powerful and magnificent way. See this and feel it and become a better Christian for it. We do not need to become pagan, but we can understand the far-reaching motives of the pagan mysteries, in that they paid their deep respect to the Almighty, but in their own natural way. Perhaps our present civilization is too aggressively superior to enter again into that old, lovely, quiet participation and admiration, that 'feeling with' life, and that deep respect, taking nothing for granted, not even the food we eat, for that has been sent to us by the great Beings of the Solar planes with the vibration of love, for understanding and nourishment.

MEDITATION

Now we will enter into the silence for a few minutes and raise these vapour-like forms of ours on wings of light to soar and merge them again for life and renewal, and enjoy again that lovely vitality and sensitive feeling, which is sent to us to use wisely, for the benefit of the whole of the Principle of Life which we serve and represent.

CHAPTER SEVEN

Density—Solids—Weight

In this part of Solar projection, we enter into an inter-dimensional zone. This is one of the many 'buffer' states between the lighter and heavier worlds. If we see dimensions as variations of density and weight, we can easily visualize that the outer space or primitive forms of life occupy much denser planes than the higher or more evolved life. This does not mean that those visiting or inhabiting the lower planes are lower Beings, but it does mean that higher forces of preparation and training are necessary for descent at times into the pressure of denser worlds, there to gather direct experience, feeling and sensation through which to be able to contribute to the raising of the denser substance into the finer matter of other worlds.

Here we begin to see that density, in the first place, is a form of control, that is there is a controlled environment that is kept in sequence and production by the various ether sub-pressures which exert upon the Planet the forces by which its atmospheres are kept in perfect sequence and harmony. This control maintains a complete Star System in balance and mathematical harmony within the Time cycle, so that it does not alter by even a second; has its appointed movements through space and keeps its rendezvous with other Stars and Systems, moving with a precision so amazing in its magnificent foresight that it humbles the human imagination to try to understand the tremendous majestic forces involved which cause this standard of continuity to exist.

Once we understand that density has a controlling function by which a dimensional life is made possible, we begin to see it also has great areas of production, and the minerals of the earth—the coal, diamonds, and oil—are all the products of the denser forces. Indeed, all fossils, fuels and the various energy levels are produced through pressure zones, and these zones are buried deep into the heart of the Planet Earth, and are treasures awaiting man's evolving requirements, to which he must eventually turn with a deeper respect than he is showing to them at the moment.

We are using up in a matter of years materials which it has taken density hundreds of thousands, even millions, of years to produce. Such is the speed up of the evolutionary process on Planetary work done by the natural laws and the weight of matter.

It is an awe inspiring thought to realize that one generation or one century should be tapping these world resources which have lain fallow, waiting for this epoch in man's evolutionary period and we should learn to respect them, not squander, fritter or plunder them or lower their design by wrong applications.

The various products of the denser world, the gases, minerals, oils and all the by-products of mineral and natural life, are there to serve the evolutionary principle, not merely to be exploited by man's laziness and ambition. It is time we began to realize that the world of density is not only highly productive but controls and produces substance, matter and change of form that make possible human life. Here we observe the rhythm of laws operating through the different pressures of densities; as we raise or lower these, so do we operate on various cycles of vibration. This is important to realize because dimensional worlds are only separated from other co-relational worlds by the density of their substance or vibration. So we have oscillation or movement in places which are indistinguishable to the natural eye, but visible on the psychic plane, an inter-dimensional relationship between density and matter which forms what we call the astral state—the intermediate or transitory state—which we pass through as we evolve to the lighter worlds.

Gravity is a great GOD-Force which keeps the world in controlled and balanced sequence, maintains the high productivity of the soil, controls environment, atmosphere, and temperature, making it possible to have an orderly world and the root system of living. Density is a form of cradle through which mankind evolves from the lower to the higher; we also see that the solids provide what we term the first root systems, upon which all production of Nature depends and by which it is anchored to the Earth's surface, which we call the 'good earth'.

We must now turn to the Solar laws to try to understand what root systems mean, for they are the product of solidity formed through pressure. This makes possible nature as we know it. We get so used to seeing trees and plants and the products of nature through her various root systems that we do not stop to realize that the potential of the root system is the basic security of the whole of the human pattern. Evolution is taking place in plant and animal, insect and bacterial life which is able to utilize the basic root systems which have been projected into the Earth's surface. This could cease because we take our food and all the things which produce it, for granted. Fertility is easily destroyed by radiation and atomic explosion and the defiling of the earth and water by these, causes a breaking-into those fields which have taken millions of years to evolve into their present efficiency, which we seem to be doing our best to destroy in one century.

Man's attitude to environment must change and a new responsibility towards it dawn, for it is not only man's background that we are dealing with, but the whole area of life force which depends to a great extent on man, who is the gateway to the higher and lighter zones and other domains of higher service and dimensional worlds. Man is a stepping stone and as the life forces are contained in his body, he represents them in sum total.

Now we must also bear in mind that we have another factor involved and that is weight. Most of our ideas as to weight, concern whether we are putting it on around the middle which gives us more to carry about. But weight holds things together in place, and in a balanced relationship to each other. It is a by-product of the density/solid world, but again, we must see this as highly productive. Weight also has its own minerals, seas of activity and its laws. So weight now becomes what we term the anchorage by which the Universe, or the place within the system of the Universe, is held in suspension or, shall we call it, oscillation.

To understand this, try to realize what a wonderful thing it is that Stars and Planets do not collide. Here we are hurtling through space at a tremendous number of miles an hour, moving through other orbits, other systems which have passed behind or in front of us, and yet we never collide. What form of attraction—what means are there—by which the Planetary systems are controlled in their rate of flow?

This is something we should know more about, for we find that it is not so much the weight as it is different energies of magnetism. This magnetic force represents what we call weight or density, with the corresponding result that we find there is a difference in relationship of one form of weight to another. What would be weight on this Planet, would not be weight on others. As soon as we remove it from its pressure zones, weight ceases to exist for it is an illusory thing, and yet without it we should not have the anchorage and the natural resources of the Earth.

The ancients knew far more about weight vibrations than we do. They were able to build pyramids with it, levitate vast columns of stone and remove them great distances by this understanding of the magnetic vibrations of weight.

Now we know from the therapeutic point of view that weight is a form of life essence in a state of change. We call it 'live' weight and 'dead' weight, and we have other descriptions for this means of recognition, yet we do not stop to recognize that weight is evolution. This form of life or 'aliveness' of earth is evolving through magnetic consciousness in various fields of creativeness.

Magnetism is a sister power to Solar energy, and it is a well known fact that sheet lightning will ripen a field of corn in hours for which days of Sunlight would be needed, and that certain magnetic flows can produce plant life out of all proportion to what we casually call weight; that bacteria and many fungi are magnetically influenced. In health or illness or any form of bodily congestion, we find that the weight ratio rises and falls with the person's consciousness. Again we are back to this weight form of balance. A person who is sick is heavy—in heart, in Spirit and in flesh. There is a certain density of matter which seems to follow such phenomena. Spiritually alive people appear light and free, they seem to have the lighter colours of the spectrum round them, while sick people have heavy, leaden, dull colours.

It seems as if there are certain projections of the human form which raises and lowers man, for his state of Being follows weight; weight is not just a question of the density of the force, it is a condition.

As we begin to realize that these various fields have different functions to perform, we can then recognize them as parts of the human and Planetary pattern and also part of the Solar projection forces which radiate into the known world.

Our work as students is to begin to understand and know more about the radiations, and to find where their relationship affects the human character and has a bearing upon human and spiritual conduct. Every seeker on the Path, everyone who seeks to know more about the Universe around them, should be aware of these resilient forces which interplay within human behaviour. We are the children of Space; we are not the victims of these things, we should become their master, but we must learn to respect them, for as friends they will serve us well, but as enemies they can appear hurtful and resentful, and thus make life very difficult by our lack of co-operation, appreciation and understanding.

These different states are also controlled by what we call the Masters of the Solar Planes. Each one of these planes of activity—and there are many—has its Sub-Masters who need to communicate with those within the Solar Planes, to make known their need of information and obtain co-ordination.

That the Gods descend to the Earth and seek to find grateful minds and Souls who will respond to their influences, seems rather far-reaching, like something out of Jules Verne, or H. G. Wells, and which is not really for us, but that is where we make a big mistake. This is not a world of imagination, but one of fact. When we enjoy good food or admire marble and precious stones, and witness the productivity of the Earth, we are witnessing the creativity of the Solar Plane influences working in the Earth. They are the resources, the products and the fruits of these systems; and these conditions and states, which we take very much for granted, are works of great wonder.

Respect for all life means that we respect what we call the root system. We are each highly productive of our particular phenomena. Each of us produces atmosphere, magnetism; each produces environmental tensions, harmonies, discords, diseases, ill-eases and through our genes we are, in a sense, manufacturing productive agents through which these forces are continually at work. We are not just a body which blows air in and out, something which walks on two legs and makes the place untidy. We are actually Solar Beings, walking, living and moving in balanced activity, creating, sharing, participating in this great mystery of unfolding evolution. And no matter how puny we may feel ourselves, or how weak and human and lost in outer space, we must now and then return to the Centre and the Root of the Principle which we represent and to which we belong.

I want to emphasize that we are all these things—we are density, and solids and weight; we are products and by-products. We are also our own creations and these are of personality and character. They are our personal environmental radiations and as such they cause diseases and disharmonies, or they work with the harmonizing forces; they are our personal vibrations. We all have certain affinities with some of these creative states more than with others.

But do realize that life is not just a question of getting up and going to work or repetition of routine. It is really participating in a great Solar experiment, and we are the Gods projected within these various between-states, experiencing and participating as Eternal Spirits, the primitive roots of the early origin of creative form. We shape, we mould, we leave behind, and it is more what we leave behind that matters, than what we find when we come.

Now to turn rather quickly—because these subjects are so vast, I can only remind you of them and encourage you to think about them—to the world of the Psyche. In various states of phenomena we find that the weight falls, that is the intermediate fields are able to manifest within a corresponding field. I have seen a fully grown man, bound to a chair, float round a room as if he were just a balloon at a party; and seen weight so reduced that an object of about half a ton could be lifted with a small finger. I have seen density, solids and stones, pass through objects in their complete and natural state and even a living bird unharmed—which was a demonstration of what we call the transcendent force.

We think of the world as solid, and if we bang our heads against a wall hard enough, we agree it has solid force, and yet under certain conditions this so-called solidity ceases to exist and then living, warm bodies of birds, fishes and people have been known and seen to pass through a wall, and coming to no harm, return to their own environment.

There is evidence of this in the Bible, such as Paul passing out of the prison by the breaking of his chains, and Peter walking through the prison gates and also the appearance of people who are seen and shown to have substance and shape and speech, who yet disappear and come and go at will. This may appear as an unusual form of transport which possibly has much to be said for it! but the point is that these things are going on all the time—that there is an inter-relationship between the solid-weight-density state and the various states surrounding it, through which they are able to pass and communicate, so making our fixed laws look ridiculous.

I remember one person who witnessed a particular type of healing and his comment afterwards was, "I must not believe this thing. If I did it makes nonsense of all my training and research, and my knowledge becomes worthless, I cannot, I must not believe this thing."

But to return to our root system. This is fixed in a certain defined weight-solid ratio system and then suddenly out of the blue comes another set of laws, and vibrations and these demonstrate that they have a power to pass over and through density and are not controlled by the weight/density/solid form that we call life. Again the Bible is full of these instances of walking through fire, of raising or ascension and the singing of the Angel choirs. We have plenty of phenomena in the ordinary Christian teachings and that of the Essenes and other esoteric schools speak of a continual relationship between worlds, of the continuous state of communication between them. So higher life becomes more or less a travelling zone between these various states of matter, and the travellers can pass to and fro and bring back full and rich memories of their experiences in the various zones of life.

I would remind you that we are not talking of something which is new and modern. We are merely referring to the basic roots of our everyday state of society; life has its proved security of fixations, but we should not become so fixed in our solid/weight ratio that we ignore the existence of other worlds and states far higher, more evolved and peopled by much more intelligent Beings than we, who have lived through various degrees of creative experience, far above our own. If we shut the door to these states of knowing, then we are isolating man in his own earth chamber, and he is losing the benefit of the wonder and majesty of all these worlds within worlds which are around us. New knowledge and awareness are the stepping stones, the way to deeper experience. But here comes the rub! We cannot expect to step out of one state of substance into another and leave behind the debris and litter of unfinished tasks. This takes us back to self-realization, self-development, self-awareness and to those wonderful zones peopled by those higher evolved Beings. We owe them a debt and also the world we are living in; the world does not owe us anything. And instead of leaving behind an impoverished world, the seeker tries to enrich the zones he has lived in, and to make it his business that he leaves behind thoughts, ideas, behaviour, creativity, freedom, happiness and hard work, that the very things he has used are the better because he has used them; the air is better because he has breathed it, and the earth he has walked upon is holy ground because he has walked on it.

As one race and nation leaves its appointed place, it should leave behind a tradition of cleanliness, usefulness and productivity. Therefore, what we do in our various zones of follow-up, which some people call 'death' is merely the stepping out of and reaching from, one zone, one state, into another. The sin of doing nothing but taking all, and giving nothing in return or leaving a religious or other body to do it all, causes more heartache than any other so-called sin, for it is a looking back rather than a looking forward. Merely to recite prayers, or to go through the motions or religion, to do no harm and certainly no good, is to live safely, and not learn to live dangerously and courageously. We can play and live so safely that we are a drag on the celestial market. We are just passengers who have not paid any fare at all!

If we encourage any religions or philosophies to be so inert, so concerned with their own salvation that they are not concerned with the evolving root systems which are their cradle, their parents, their mother; if we think we can isolate ourselves from the cradle of birth and ignore it, then we must not be surprised if that very cradle turns back on us and causes us trouble. Such periods of remorse, as we pass from density substance in one realm to another, is a thing I want none of you to experience, but rather that our comings and going may be rich in self-realization and the development of the spiritual ego in the environment of ideas. To have the courage to live what we believe, and to use our life in some form of developed service, is the least we can do, and as we enrich these various fields by our life, so will these fields enrich us by their participation in our evolving life force.

So this is partnership all the way, partnership of the Heavens, the skies, the waters, the good earth, the plants, the treasures of the soil, the food and the products of all these things which give us the joy of living. We must approach them with a deep respect, joy and gratitude, and give to them what we would give to a child who brought us a daisy chain. We would never say crudely: "Take that silly thing away." We would enter into the mind of the child and say, "It is a beautiful daisy chain. It is a lovely thing." Sometimes a child is nearer to the level of nature than adults, and if we could go back again to some of the pleasures of our childhood and remember the first cave we went into, the first time we saw the full moon, or heard a wonderful fairy tale, or were frightened and were comforted and held close by someone, we might also return to that level. But go back we must, and find these treasures and give them to someone who has lost their love, respect and desire.

MEDITATION

So now in our Meditation, I want you to definitely feel a sense of belonging and partnership —a partnership with an active evolving wonderful Universe, peopled by and associated with highly evolved Beings who are brothers, sisters and full partners on the way to this great unfoldment of the Life pattern.

And try to add a sense of treasure, and in that nearness you will find you become lighter, are more creative, your health will improve, your roots and system, your function, and your body, will all respond to a lighter feeling, a flow of vitality.

In other words, we become in tune with the living forces of the Solar planes, and by doing that we are bringing them into a nearer and closer relationship to our environment and other people's lives, and set in motion the pattern of things to come.

CHAPTER EIGHT

Thought—Architect and Builder

Here we pass from the contemplative to the meditative stage, and I want first to deal with what we term the Principle of Evolution in revelation of detail and the means by which man is exposed to the different relationships of Truth. As his capacity develops so his state of reality increases and the reality in Truth is man's capacity to absorb. This can be achieved by an internal awareness of an external event and we have here the composite picture of an internal and an external world force competing for the attention and life force of an individual. On one hand we have the mystical, the Soul force; on the other we have the human and the psychological forces. Man is passing from the stage of material pressures, that is, where it is necessary to fight for his survival, into the stage where he must struggle for fulfilment, and these stages are the cycles by which evolution exerts its various pressures.

On the one hand we have the idea of material, or the psychological ownership, by which security, success and ambition are taught as a feature of man's behaviour. On the other hand we see developing slowly and surely a psycho-social pressure which is exerting a new type of influence. This is causing a revision of many of the old concepts and values, and man is beginning to realize that ownership can become a burden which holds back the evolution of his Spirit. The psycho-evolution is bringing forward a new concept of reality and a different approach to man's relationship with the Universe. Man has, up to now, considered it necessary only to serve his own survival needs, but there are new developments, showing that man is not only a part of the great Cosmic evolution, but that this planet is keyed into the evolution of all other systems, therefore linked to Cosmic timing. Thus evolution is not Planetary only, it is a Universal concept in movement. This lifts us above the trivial, the mundane, the physical approach to thinking. It means that we must live on this horizon of thought, right out into space, and extend ourselves beyond the horizon of time and begin to think of the human race and man's destiny as a fulfilment into a new metier, a New Age.

This great change, by which the thought patterns are re-manifesting themselves on another plane, means that the psycho or Soul force, the Soul evolutionary pressures, are bringing about a state of self-awareness, a self-adjustment, and self-responsibility. In all the original Esoteric schools this question of the psycho-pressures, that is psycho-evolution through social behaviour, was heralded as the approach to a New Age, where thought would not flow merely from human thinking but would join in the great Cosmic flow of new dimensional creativeness. For this reason we can see these signs of the external pressures almost forcing man to reach beyond his own Planet in time where, though he has tremendous problems at his own doorstep, he is still imaginative enough to reach out to the Stars. In fact, the great challenge to mankind is his imperfection and his ignorance, and by these two forces man can raise himself to a mental stature and creative Being far beyond his present ideas of human realization. We see that the evolutionary pressure has three main stages:

(1) That which we call the mechanical system which man copies in all his engineering and creative art.
(2) The chemical worlds which man exploits.
(3) The plant and animal worlds of which man has the use.

For as he uses these basic evolutionary materials and systems for his thought worlds, as stepping stones to new phases, it is in these intellectual imaginative fields that the psycho-evolution or revolution is taking place and putting its stresses and strains on every system that man has made.

As we look again at these systems we find their immobility and resistance to change has been man's greatest destructive force. As individuals we would not kill, but as a system we would exterminate. As a system becomes a social order under pressure of nationalism we are quite prepared to annihilate another nation when, individually, we probably would even regret to kill a fly. Man enslaves himself in these systems which he forms around himself to such an extent that he loses his identity and because the systems are so steeped in tradition and repetition he loses his freedom to think and act.

The New Age, or the new revolution of thought, must be free from the terrible scourges of famine and poverty, useless suffering, ridiculous over-abundance of material things and from the wastage of resources in unnecessary projects which only have nationalism, pride and the old survival instincts; free from the armament race, which is imprisoning and tying man down to the very soil, the minerals and the plants of the earth.

It is to the mystical schools that we turn eventually for the revolution in thinking. It was to the Greeks and the Romans, to the Egyptians and the great forces of Atlantis in their spiritual heyday that the epochs of new thought constructions were projected, and at present this great tension of thinking is causing an unrest, and unravelling of many of the old concepts. In fact, our attitude to change must be an acceptance of continuity, for on this human survival depends. Often in human relationships this sense of continuity is lost. It has become enshrouded in the fear of darkness and death, fear of disease, insecurity, immaturity and so on, where the continuity is not convincing enough. We are not convinced that we are a part of an evolving Cosmos or that man is a God in a state of awakening, being forged and made in the great destiny of Time and Planetary experience. It is his pettiness, his smallness, his meanness by which man ties himself to his sufferings and his miseries; and his lack of courage and adventure that causes him to become the craven creature that the lower thought force has caused him to imitate. It is to the visionary intellectual imagination that we turn to find a new impulse and it is in the regulation of exterior thought to the interior life that we see the schools of teaching are beginning to bend their power. It is always the few who sway the many, and in most of the schools of thought in the metaphysical world these new eras of thinking are being born and we accept them today more easily than we did, say, twenty years ago. We question tradition without spoiling it, we look at orthodoxy and see its mistakes; we view religions in a new sense of transparency and we can see human relationships in a detached and impartial way.

Thought is the architect and the builder; thought precedes creation and so creation is the child of thought, the free imagination which links itself to the impulse of the original idea.

The difficulty—apart from man's inability to change and the fixation of his system—is the fact that in the old psychological pattern of thinking we are governed by this rather unhappy way of thought of profit and loss, and to every measure of interest or advantage, loss and gain or reward seems to have been, up to now, the deciding factor of its worth. That is psychological thinking, but when we pass to psycho-thinking in the psycho-evolutionary pattern, we find we no longer think in ideas of loss, gain and reward. We must see ourselves as God-Beings on a great Planetary adventure, passing through Time and Space in this complex and mysterious force called Eternity, and for that reason we begin now to free ourselves from the imprisonment of bodies, systems and mechanical contrivances, so that the thought forces can launch themselves freely into a new dimension. Unless vision is re-born man will again descend to the depths, but evolution only allows man to descend so far into his lower patterns before pressure and the exertion of life-force stirs him to new activities. At the moment I feel that all metaphysical schools and teaching have a new responsibility in opening their doors to ideas, and in their general thinking to embrace world events; to bring into a new relationship every experience, and transmit them into positive thinking. Mankind is the only Being who can transmit experience and it is through this transmission—through the soul-Force—that the new relationship will be formed. It is not until this begins to enter our life that we see destiny being fulfilled, and realize that survival is not so necessary but our evolutionary responsibility is much greater. When we see that our journey is to the Stars and not the graveyard, and that we are not merely human Beings full of aches and pains, but that we are Gods in the making, being prepared for the great unfoldment of the Cosmic future, it should bring the sense of a new reality and reduce the meanness and trivialities which govern our lives today. Men have said before that when a nation loses its vision it loses its future. This is quite true. So it is not to the world of the politician, nor of the psychologist or their ways of valuation that we turn for the salvation of thought and the architectural construction of new worlds, it is to the metaphysical, the mystic, the visionary.

The terms to which we have become accustomed over the years are beginning to creep into medical and physical sciences. What was often looked upon as dreams and make-believe and odd prophecies are beginning to take on a new type of revelation, a new meaning in the laboratories; and in research, the great intellectual field by which man is groping into the invisible world, he is discovering new spectrums, new forces and powers. He is entering into a dimensional relationship that he has never known before; therefore it is not from the leaders of the religions that this great force of new thinking will be produced, it will come from those who realize the importance of Soul-participation in the discovery of the unseen worlds.

As, on the one hand, we have the scientist in his laboratory so, on the other, we have the human Being in the laboratory of life. Here are being forged and moulded into personalities, characters and values far beyond our present needs. Here in the time-space consciousness we experience birth and death, heat and cold, loss and gain, and slowly but surely we are stripped of many of the old physical values which bind us to the world, and we are being guided—almost prodded—into a new concept of reality. This is where the esoteric teaching—the psycho-evolution as we call it—is beginning to fill the gap between the

known and the unknown. We know from our therapeutic research that illness is mainly spiritual, and that some diseases
and discords inflicted on the human body have their origin in
thought structures, past lives and future destinies; that no event
is merely an event in itself, it is in relationship to the whole
evolutionary experience and has an important contribution, no
matter how trivial, in the forging of a new world.

Once we become absorbed in Soul participations, much of
the sense of loss and tragedy begin to retreat. Fear of death becomes less and it is not the promise of a future life in luxury
that is held before us, it is a life filled with the development of
a highly interesting and exciting future. On the other hand,
we know that lack of Soul participation weakens the physical
force and the mind. It is when we have Soul and mind working
as a tangible means of communication that we shall forge new
people, new systems and new ideas.

The flow of a new world is coming from a dimension above
us—it will not flow from the dimension below us—it is in
those who reach out to this higher realm and are prepared to
receive from these new stations of thinking a form of relationship which requires the lessening of the personality and the
increase of Soul participation.

This is where the architect of thought comes in, because we
are very reluctant to surrender our personality to a higher intelligence or to impressions of thinking which seem beyond
our own. So difficult is it that perhaps this is where the Soul
force meets its greatest battle. What are these personalities?
They are usually made up of the lesser humanities, pride and
envies, jealousies and hates, loves and desires, ambitions, and
other things which we need not mention here. These are
dimensional products of our survival patterns and it is the surrender of these patterns, to enter on to the path of fulfilment,
that causes man's greatest tragedy and self-misery. But when
we surrender this third-dimensional aspect and concept and
accept the higher dimensional values, meanings and purposes
they slowly invade these lesser forces; and with constant work
and self-observation we can reduce them to some form of con-

trol, so that death no longer looms over us, nor does age threaten us, disease and illness are not a persecution and life itself is an adventure in Time and Space instead of an existence waiting for the end.

There is a great hopelessness and hunger in the outer world — because man is so caught up with his external abundance that he swamps himself by the trivialities of that abundance. Much of it is unnecessary and unwanted; it has a nuisance value, it becomes a debt, an onus, it is a weight upon man's shoulders inflicting monetary penalties and social demands. This perhaps is where Communism and many other of the singular social forces seek to gather some strength, but nothing is gained by surrendering individuality to a State where thought is controlled and forced loyalties are extracted. These things are not evolution. They are man's pressure against his fellows, forcing them into the downward path. These powers exist because of the fear in the humand mind. The more fears we have the more we can be imprisoned and enslaved. We should not be afraid of starvation and death, persecution and poverty, because the fear of these things is not urgent upon us. New visions, a new sense of reality can free us from these whips, these scourges. Occasionally we enter into a moment of truth, where the test of the metaphysical thought collides with the tragedy of human thinking. Death may come our way, tragedy appear upon the path and the whole rhythm of life may seem to be displaced, but here again we must see that strength can be procured through exposure, and by being exposed to the action of thoughts, works and experiences we shall forge new thinking systems, new mechanisms and a new approach.

Now let us turn to the individual side of the architect of the future, because that is what we are. We are building the New Age by the status of our thought life now. Creation is thought which has been projected into material, and the strange thing about thought is that it is not an instantaneous thing, it may have a delayed force, and for that reason sometimes it deceives us into thinking we are getting away with something, because the bill is not presented immediately! Nature delays presenting us with the bill of our errors and our mistakes and the Gods in their compassion forgive us a great deal of our misadventures, but it does not alter the fact that because there is this delay in time, that the results of our thinking will not produce fruit. You hear it said, "But these people have money, they have power, position; they have everything and have broken every rule of the book, and look at them, they are fit and well, healthy and rich!" "Yes," we can say quietly, "and they may be thoroughly miserable and unhappy, lonely and scared of life and of death." So, on the one hand we have the psychological possessions, and on the other the spiritual sense of freedom, but let us go further here and realize the building stage of every life. We said before it takes 40 years to live out the mistakes of other people's imposition and 40 years to live out our own, and I think most of us are getting to the stage when we can have an adventure with our own ideas, instead of working out our grandparents' and past systems of education. In fact, as we enter into the maturer pattern we should have more fun because we have less to lose. This sense of age should retreat into a sense of maturity, that is the quality of thinking. When the main responsibilities of the family have decreased we can enter into the adventure with ideas and begin to put them into action. Now ideas produce energy, ideas produce health, thought is good for the heart and the circulation. A thinking mind does not grow old, it always smells sweet, but a mind which goes to sleep produces an offensive odour; it is awful! There is a certain sense of sweetness, niceness, cleanness, aliveness, in a mind and Soul which is working, but there is a smell of death in the mind that has gone to sleep and a body that is waiting for decay. Therefore, in a world which is frightened of decay, morally afraid of death and which insists on its fixed systems, codes and ideas, we can go in and set free this part of life with a new excitement and a new measure. In fact we are undertaking to be our own best friend and nobody need worry. I remember when I was a boy I had some good friends and we played for a long time together, then somebody came to me and said, "You know, you ought not to play

86

with those children, they are the Undertaker's children." And it suddenly struck me—what a silly thing to say! As far as I was concerned the undertaker was only a carpenter, and how could his children be tainted with the blemish of death because their father was a sanitary engineer of human bodies? And we continued to play, but I noticed that a lot of children did not play with them. So you see it is not only racial prejudice that can spoil children's lives, it is social orders and the impediment of age-old thinking of the parents which causes distortion of the child's mind.

It does not take long to step over the fixed picture of ideas before you are in collision with the insinuating methods of reducing originality and clear thinking into a stage of almost witchcraft, paganism and other impositions which religion, in its fixation, has inflicted upon the human race. There is hardly a school of thought or place, whether it is the activities of a child's mind or what we eat and how we think, that has not been affected. It is the structure that we make by our thinking textures which is going to decide the world of the future. Therefore, unless we can stir those who will have an adventure and a rendezvous with new ideas, there is small hope. We shall go on perpetuating war, pestilence, famine, pain, poverty and waste. So the psyche—or Soul—revolution is the only means by which mankind will enter into a new relationship, first with himself, then with his world and then with the Planetary and other systems of the great Cosmos, of which he is an important, living, active partner. It is rather humbling to think that our thoughts and constructions on this Planet can affect events on another Planet which may be in light years many millions of miles away. Because thought is not restricted to a dimension nor is it restricted to light or dark. Thought is a universal language, a universal power. In fact, every word we know is the projection of some great thought for us, and Genesis is not far wrong when it sees the great projection of thought-force cycles impinging upon Planetary forces and moulding and shaping them into forms, colours and systems that we know today. Therefore, thought is the builder; not only can it be the builder of our present systems and a challenge to the things which cause us to destroy and deny each other the freedom of thinking, but it seems to me that we are the representatives of a New Age, a New Age of thought and in our conversation, the things we write, or our attitudes, our quietness, our sureness, our inner convictions, our sense of serenity and sense of prosperity, our generosity, our forgiveness, our deeper vision and our wider sense of things, is the material which will precede the New Age.

So see yourselves definitely as thought forces ensouled in time for as long as the Soul—the Psyche—is able to work with the mind, great things can happen. And bear in mind that in the things that we are, even our ordinary social relationships, we are laying foundations for new thought worlds—not as noisy revivalists but by being quietly ourselves. Here we see how new epochs, new generations, new societies are formed by a slow infiltration of new dimensional thinking, a new concept of continuity, a refreshing idea of Christianity, a widening and deepening of the knowledge of the old religions, an awakening of responsibility to the new forces of Science and a deeper understanding of the psychological conditions of human behaviour. There must also be a deepening and an enriching of human affairs, in our conduct, how we think, what we do and say, realizing that these things *are* of another world; they are being brought from those spheres to the place upon the earth where we, as builders, are actually constructing new worlds by the infiltration or the sending out of the higher concepts. So we slowly begin to enter into the psycho-revolution; the Soul beginning to come into its own and linking itself with its partner, the mind, is able to transform and change and be a new force in the world, and that force, that new world, is being created by individuals. It is this personal, gentle, rich and wonderful thinking which helps to give us courage and strength when we feel afraid, tired and weary. For this part of our time-space consciousness is so short that when we shall look back upon it in the light of years, and see these very short dwellings in the destiny of time, and review the structures we have left behind, we shall see the seeds we have sown and have the destiny of evolution working out through human contributions. Then will be the time that we shall be richly blessed for any inconvenience we may have suffered here, any so-called loss or any gain that we think we may have missed, because the enrichment through the personality of the Spirit is something so wonderful, so new and enlivened, so active and beautiful, that we cannot afford to let it down, for the sake of the few who gave up their comfort—even their lives to launch a new concept of Eternity and the purpose of man's human destiny towards his GOD.

MEDITATION

Now let us be quietly in meditation, and try to feel this true sense of destiny and fulfilment, to free ourselves from the small personality and enter into this deeper relationship with the great Universe which is our friend, our companion, our world of Being. This is our life.

CHAPTER NINE

Colour—Fragrance—Form

It is at this stage that we have to merge the Solar plane with the Cosmic. We speak of the Solar Sun as one dimension and the Cosmic Sun as another, but we must realize that the common denominator between all dimensions is Light, and in this common field exists the permanent or Eternal link between every plane of activity throughout the entire Cosmos, the link by light-waves. On the one hand we have Solar light which develops radiation, heat and friction; on the other hand there is Cosmic light, which develops no heat or friction but interpenetrates at all levels and has a universal passport which can reach the very depths of darkness and pass through, whereas the Solar forces are more restricted to the surface chemistry of the Earth. The Sun is a tremendous atomic furnace suspended in space, radiating vast magnetic, electrical and other energy fields, much of which affects our fluid atmosphere, that is, it moves entire oceans of water throughout the earth. Every sea, river and ocean is a living part of the Sun energy of Life. It is perpetual motion as we know it, but it is also the parent of all growth which depends entirely upon the nourishment it can absorb, first through its Solar parent and second, through its Cosmic counterpart.

To understand light we must also realize that the interdimensional factor of light is due to its intensity, and intensity is what we recognize as form and colour. First then, colour is the refractory, that is the intermediate vibrations of the white light, and it has its semblance in so-called energy fields. When we look at colour we are really looking at a blue-print of the various energies which are activated in the lower substance of matter itself. We can better understand this if we realize that light can transmute matter, that is, it is able to change the substance of all forms of creation and completely alter its nature, environment, climate and creative use. We see light as the great transmuter, the transformer of foods from light energies into light fields; then we begin to see that the sense of vision, light, colour and sound, is the world of reality, while the world we feel, of sensory form is merely a denser level on which we move temporarily and have our Being.

As we enter the subtle worlds where the new language is being spoken and new horizons are being unfolded, we should realize that air, colour and breath are all equal. Once we see that breath is the form by which colour and fragrance are able to transmit or communicate, the breath of life becomes the origin of life.

In occult schools Initiates were taught to live through fragrance or breath, the idea being that once they were able to contact the Cosmic breath or cosmic energy, their need for physical foods were practically nil; they were able to live through the intake of breath or fragrance. It may be difficult to think that we can make a meal off the scent of a rose or that the wonderful aroma of nature at work is as good as a plate of strawberries and cream, but the strange thing is that fragrance and colour are definitely nourishment. For this we turn to the chemical world and the digestion, because the digestion is the world of transmutation, the change of one form of substance to another. Here we find that if the fragrance of the food is in vibration with that of the mind, the food has a very high nutritional value. If the fragrance is below our vibration, its energy ratio in transference is exceedingly low. This gives us a little insight into the old esoteric teaching of the holy breath, living through breath, fragrance and colour. The fact of transmutation, the chemical change of substances influenced by scent, leads us to another interesting occult observation—that all things have scent. We may have thought that perfume belongs to the flower world but actually character has its own aroma, a mood has a perfume and temperament its own smell. Fear has an acid smell, and animals can smell this and will attack fear because they themselves are afraid of it. It is this language of aroma and fragrance, of form and taste, which communicates an invisible need of nourishment which is always linked with thought. If you can think of thought and nourishment as the same thing you realize it is the smell of the food we eat which increases its vitamin content and nutritional value, and we can visualize the essences involved in that breath are actually substantiating the etheric forces within the body. Now this may be a little difficult, but try to realize that scents and gases are suspended density, which means that the gaseous world has not yet solidified and some of it never will. We live in a world of nourishment, of magnesiums and phosphates, calcium and irons, all in the air. We drink water which is a combination of two gases, plus forms of aerial nourishments which, together, will feed all the fluid chemicals of the body, so the amount of dense food we need for nourishment is really very small, but the amount of food and nourishment which we absorb through breathing, sound and colour is remarkably high. This is beginning to open up quite new ideas. Of course in mental sickness therapists have suspected for a long time that a grey or black and white world produces a sickness of its own. We cannot bear to think of a world of only black and white, and it would not be so much a question of optical loss as of nutritional loss.

Now as we see this in relation to the body, we must also see it as a nutritional factor to the Soul, for the Soul's food is also colour, sound, form and scent. It has been said that the Cosmic essence flows from the heart to the glands. This is quite true. Colour therapy is a small indication that this is possible, and though our range of colours on the third dimension is still crude we use colour therapy as a reliable means of re-energizing depleted fields. Each of us has an entirely different key of vibrations, what would soothe one would be antagonistic to another; what would warm one would chill another. So our colour fields, our colour zones, energies and fragrance are like our fingerprints—identical to ourselves. But there are certain Universal colour fields or nourishments to which we can apply the science of occult thinking, and this the old Alchemists used to distil, from the flowers the essence of health, and from nature the aroma of healing.

We try in all occult and esoteric studies to become more familiar with the subtle, for the unrevealed, that which is barely detected, the trace-elements almost, do the work. The massive dose, the big range of colour, the great field of green or expanse of blue sky has a certain universal backcloth, but it is not in that field the energies are released. There is more energy released in Sunrise and Sunset and times of rainbows than perhaps in any other way. I know somebody who, whenever there was a rainbow imminent used to feel very excited, would tingle all over and look at the sky and wait—and they were never wrong. It seemed as if they had a subtle indication that a rainbow had a communication with them on its colour frequency. We know that the basic colours of the rainbow are those of all artists' mixtures, from which they can create any shade, pastel or otherwise, that it is possible to make. But that is at a mechanical level.

We are trying to deal with this now at an esoteric level and this is where we can do some real work. I said before that character has a scent, that mood has odour, that the temperament of thought also has a perfume, in loss of temper another odour emanates. Try to realize that all these different perfumes, like whole sets of colours, mingle above the head so that we live under the canopy of this aromatic essence, good, bad or neutral, and it is in a constant state of change. Animals and children are very aware of this. Children especially will take little notice of a body-smell but can be attracted to a person who may look quite unclean outside but whose inner smell appeals to them. You see, it is not always the visual factor that appeals, it is the subtle emanation, the implied inference by which the energy forces communicate or transmute. Remember, light is the law of transmutation. Keep that firmly in mind as we proceed along this pathway and begin to see that creation is different light-forms in degrees of colour, in various grades of scent, having power energies which release or feed certain patterns of creative force. We notice that the plant life has what we call a controlled time sequence. So do we. Now a plant is controlled entirely by the length of its absorption of solar energy, for the Solar life controls the time when the snowdrops come, when the lilies and the roses appear. We are actually witnessing the Solar-clock light and the plant is responding to the length and type of light energy which is being transmitted at that particular time of year; thus we have our Spring or Autumn plants and blossoms, which their perfume and colours, all a part of the changing Cosmic and Solar energy, radiating into the world of substance and giving it its varied change and form.

We can now see that light is the master pattern through which the subtle, the beautiful, the lovely, the gracious, flow into and beautify while at the same time bringing a new measure of creativeness. We know how it is possible to start with an ordinary dog-rose and gradually build it up until we have a flower of lovely colour and perfume and beautiful shape. Man has been able to raise the consciousness of the dog-rose to the full consciousness of that beautiful piece of artistry in which he has co-operated with the forces of light and has produced, with the aid of these natural forces, a wonderful perfume, a lovely colour, a new pattern of creation. In other words, a new form has been established with man's participation.

Since that can happen to a rose—or any other flower, it follows that this same thing can happen to character. We know that character and environment or climate, have a certain antagonistic relationship, and we are beginning to suspect that this involvement between atmosphere, climate and environment can cause division of the colour frequency of a person's character. This we call environmental displacement and in children it is recognized as one of the ways in which they can become child delinquents; this can be because they have lost their parents, or have no security or fixed pattern of youth, but the strange thing is, it is not this at all. There are many cases of children who have lived in abominable homes and yet love is there amongst all the dirt, and a warmth within the poverty. It seems that this 'rose' can survive even the most difficult circumstances and still have a fragrance, an individuality and character.

This leads us into a new analysis of what we call human behaviour. There are some science fiction writers who are even going so far as to say that the scientists of the future will develop certain perfumes and colours that will be able to control the responses and reactions of the population, so that instead of the Police force they are going to try to control us by good and bad smells! They are actually doing that now, but in a rather different way. The supposition is feasible because it was found that certain forms of electronic discharges definitely made people moody, co-operative or bad-tempered. In one case they experimented with a high frequency set by the side of a scientist. If you have smelt high frequency you will know the effect is like burnt ozone. Well, we know that these ozone odours are particularly vicious. I cannot stand them very long myself, but they are now being used in skin hospitals and people with severe burns rest in the ozone-created atmosphere, which helps to keep them free from pain and reduces the need for dressings. The extraordinary fact is that the odour, the electrical radiation, is healing the skin and isolating the pain nerve, with no physical or visible contact at all—just the aroma of the magnetic and ozone-gas field.

We are also aware that in the basic nature of human behaviour there are certain, what we call, retaliatory colours. Red, of course, is often used or depicted as the colour of anger and of danger. Actually that is not so. It has been used for that because its spectrum of penetration is the highest we know in our atmosphere; in other words of all the colours put at a distance, red would be distinguishable because of its wavelength more than any other. But actually the red zones are the zones of creative love. They are the permanent centres of creativity, fertility, home, motherhood, family, affection, warmth, circulation and the heart; all these are part of the red zone spectrum and are not a suspect or dangerous thing as we have used

95

it in our mechanical application, which has given us what we call 'colour associations.' Now these associations are also linked with perfume and many of you no doubt can go back into your childhood and remember when your mother was baking bread or making jam, or whatever aroma happened to strike you at that time, and you will never forget it. Maybe it was a lavender hedge as you walked up to the house, perhaps the smell of new mown hay or even, as one friend of mine used to say, "All I need to make me happy is the smell of onions frying in the pan." It reminded him of the home and comfort of his mother, of a warm kitchen, of well-cooked food and family round him. He had only to fry onions and the whole association of that thought and the rather strong smell —lodging-house smell, I used to call it! would come again and he would feel well and at peace and in harmony with the world. Even the smell of onions, apparently, has a therapeutic effect!

Now to consider what we call chemical reactions to colour, perfume and sound. This may interest people who suffer from hay fever or catarrh and other forms of chemical reaction to perfume and scent. It should be realized by those who feel the incoming perfume, scent or aroma which causes any form of irritation that, in many cases, it is not the scent or the aroma which is causing the irritation, it is the thought picture associated with it. So really, in all forms of basic conditions such as hay fever or catarrh we can alleviate the mechanical side to quite an extent, but if we could discover the thought-force that was released when that particular odour or penetrating colour was in evidence, we could release the thought and thus free the chemical reaction on the glands, because that is exactly what hay fever and catarrh and sinus trouble is, congestion, but on a subtle level.

Light is the means by which the glands convert food, and when we have too much of one food and not enough of another, it means that the conversation chemistry of the individual is either working plus or minus, but it is also affected by a thought-association attached to that period or time, to that aroma or scent. A simple example of this—I spoke of onions

96

and you almost smelt them, if I speak of lemons your mouths begin to water, and if I were to suck a lemon you would feel your saliva beginning to flow, and also visualize the lemon in my hand.

The effect of this is what we call chemistry-association to scent, perfume, to colour and to sound. It actually has a strong physical response. This is revealing because it shows that the body is not so much being controlled by the bulk of food that we eat as by the fragrance, the life-forces involved in conjunction with the sense-memory in which that scent has been applied. With most cases of sinus trouble we find there has been somewhere in the history of that life an emotional sacrifice, and the Soul has had to do without something that it desperately needed. Now hunger has an emotional content. For instance, an unhappy person usually eats a lot. A frustrated person is inclined to drink a lot—tea mostly—ask any Civil Servant! It is not the fluid but the sound of the teacups and the spoons which is doing the job! It would be disappointing if you did not get the fluid afterwards, but the association, the mouth-watering, the psychological release, the moment you can lift your head, take your shoulder off the wheel, and psychologically not be accused of laziness, in that moment of respite the Soul comes into its own for a fraction of a minute, and life becomes momentarily pleasant.

Some people eat little and yet put on weight; others eat a lot and never put on weight at all—much to the envy of the others of course. This again is in direct relationship to light, colour, fragrance and sound, because we are noticing a distinct glandular pattern reaction which is actually affecting the shape or form. So when you look at the minuses and pluses, remember that the shape or form, the fragrance, the nourishment, the food, is the transmutation of certain light rays which have various energy reactions, such as love, hate, resentment, insecurity, fear and so on, and all these things have a perfume. Now this was always taught to the esoteric students before they went on what they called their mission, or their journey. They were sent off for five to seven years in which to put to the test all they had been taught. They were to go out into the world with nothing but their knowledge, their observation and the innermost knowing that the Spirit of creation was within self. They were expected to go out into harvest fields that would not produce, and make them grow; to go into barren lands and help to bring abundance; to go into famine, ill-health, misery and plague and there bring health, balance, and reason. In other words, they were sent out to use their powers in the world of density; and on their return they were able to show that they had passed their Initiations as they moved through the plagues, the storms and tempests, the heat and cold, for they were able to manifest and bring harmony, abundance or control back into these various zones of creativity. The Christ did this in many simple ways, He told the weather to behave quietly, the storm to cease, the sea to be calm. He did it in a purely conversational way as if anybody could do it, and the forces obeyed. In other words, they were responsive to the command of the Initiate.

This occult and esoteric knowledge, creation and change of form, the secrets of light, nourishment and transmutation were the basic teachings of all the early religions. When Abraham found water he was merely doing what was possible as one who was in complete accord with the water spirits, and was able to manifest this law even in the desert. The mirage is a rather daunting phenomena to see in the middle of the desert— see streams and mountains and waterfalls—draw near and they disappear. Actually the true disciple-Initiate should be able to go into the landscape and actually create those conditions. We do not really need bulldozers and contractors and so on. In some of the backward countries it is found better to send one good man with simple "know how" to live, work and teach the people, than it is to send a lot of food and machinery; the people must be taught to create for themselves.

Now such a man will not only use his particular knowledge but, as a servant of evolution, will draw on his esoteric, spiritual, Solar and Cosmic background, and if it is deep enough people will listen to him; if it is not they will probably ignore him.

98

The reaction, the response between the communication of those primitive people and their teacher will depend on his sincerity, his genuineness, and his ability to demonstrate that he has obtained dominion over those particular forces which have previously enslaved them, and is for that reason, able to transmute, change and increase their abundance, for ignorance and superstition are barriers to the Greater Life.

As we begin to visualize this line of esoteric work we see that living it is not a question of making life more comfortable by keeping tradition and custom alive or ignoring our problems, but that the whole life force—good and bad—is manifesting group transmutation, and that events are part of the life principle in action. The purpose of this special work is to stir up the latent knowledge, the pre-knowledge that is already in each consciousness, to release that pre-knowledge and bring it into action now. This requires great patience and a lot of uncovering. Throughout our many lives we may have put layers over this ancient wisdom; perhaps distorted and mis-used it, over-used or under-used it, and for that reason, as the Prayer Book says, "There is no health in us." But in spite of all these experiments or abuses we are training the vehicle of creation through sight and scent, through taste and form, and through thought. In other words, we are all Initiates on the Path, making his or her errors, making experiments, going out and about to challenge and work with the first Principle of Life, from which eventually emerges the Gods and the Masters and the Initiate workers of the future. It is not only now that we enter into the market place, the school of life for deeper searching, we have been this way before on the quest of internal light, the Light of Truth.

Up to now we have spoken only of Solar and Cosmic light. Now I want to draw your attention to what we call the Etheric light. The Etheric light is Cosmic light which has been transmuted by the Spirit within. Remember, when we eat ordinary food it has to be converted into energy and warmth, and the same thing happens with Cosmic food. We first have the conversion of Solar energies through the glands. We then get the conversion of the Cosmic energies which are higher creative forces and which, through the Soul's Spirit activity or chemistry, are converted into what we call, for the sake of explanation, Etheric light. This is a very rare and beautiful light and its home is many dimensions above us, but every Soul sent forth from the great Cosmic Centre is given this divine chemistry, this ability to create and use Etheric light. It is above all other light forces; by its power to transmute, to change, to convert, it has its place in the highest creative ethers and, in special circumstances, the Initiates of Christ could change flesh and cells, precede time, overcome gravity and be able to work in a manifested field so remarkable and instantaneous as to be called miraculous. It was this etheric God-light which was transmuting and reflecting itself onto the body-life forces of the individual, revitalizing them so that they became physically etherically active and, therefore, able to throw out all the impurities in the body, remove deformities of character, to re-mould and re-shape the whole mood and temperament, and re-form and restore the many levels of life forces to their original pattern.

We have all of us strayed a long way from our original pattern, believe me! As life ebbs away we make our experiments with living—not all of them wise—and by the nature of things 'err and stray' from the Path, but basically, that true and original pattern is constant, is always there, and in spiritual therapeutic work the results are often due to this being revealed. Concentrated etheric power lights up a person's etheric lamp for them, even bringing to their body a glow that will shine around them. Such radiance will strengthen the heart, cast out fear; it will change the present and transmute the past, for the intensity of this light can purify and cleanse many false values which have accumulated, due to the lack of the internal light which would normally keep the body-house clean and wholesome, well balanced and spiritually fed. This of course is reaching up to high therapeutic values but eventually this New Age work, this bringing of the miracle to the ground level, will become accepted as natural. This Etheric light force can be brought to bear even into an almost decomposed body and enable it to re-shape the whole cellular pattern, to re-group glandular functions, reconstitute bone structure and restore body purity approximately to its original design. This is a star —a challenge to man's future thinking.

One day we shall look back on many of these bodies and forms and shapes that we have made and view them with, I hope, not too much shame, but with more spiritual thought; perhaps we could have done better, but the point to remember is, we shall be looking back at our denser bodies from a purer form and fragrance, and some of the muddy, grey, ugly things which show as desire in our thought-force colour patterns will not appear very beautiful. However we are in a state of becoming and we must not wait for Etheric perfection, for in the meantime we can learn to use the Solar, the Cosmic and eventually, the Etheric Light, so at this stage in our progress it is the awakening to this consciousness that is important.

The esoteric moral we can draw from this picture is that we are children of Light; we are composed and fed from it. Its various fragrances are different vibrations and its various colours are different frequencies and, together, it forms—us— we are this Living Light pattern emerging through evolution to high places. Many of the old Masters who came back to write some of the original music tried to bring back the pure form of music as it was known. Some great artists tried to depict this subtle message in colour and shape in their artistry. Some reached out to recapture this original purity in many experiments of architecture. Initiates entered into earth at different times to re-introduce their skills in pure creativity, leaving for posterity a master classic which all other efforts could be measured and fortified from. The Christ is the greatest of these, when He says "The works that I do shall he do also, and greater works than these shall he do." This means that this same force, same power is apparent, this power of transmutation through the law of light, colour, sound, form and thought are as much for us today—in fact more so—than they were in the denser, cruder, more primitive times of a few thousand years ago. Evolution and light in the last century have stepped up the quality of conscious living so high, that in a hundred years we have over-stepped five thousand years and that, you will admit, is a very quick speed-up in evolutionary time-force. Man is now allowed to use electricity, having progressed from his oil lamps and his tapers and from the fats and butter of animals; soon his great atomic and hydro-electricity programmes, and the actual generation of power from the sea, will bring night and day together. How much we now regulate our lives by electricity is brought home to us when we consider that we only need a power cut to feel how helpless we are in our modern age without artificial light. It is a little reminder of how highly dependent we are upon the forces of light, for on light depends our creativity, our comfort, our security, the whole welfare of communal and physical life, as we know it, is dependent entirely upon generating and using light forces that have their birth in Solar and Cosmic sources.

So that in quickening the consciousness through light, we must also become aware that sound and colour, fragrance and form are also being stepped up. The result is that people today are getting more sound conscious than they were and noise is becoming an attack upon the supersensitivity of the awakened, evolving consciousness, due to this tremendous pressure of evolution in the past hundred years. The thing to remember is that we are part of this great century of awakening. We have come here to share and participate in it, so it is not for us merely to be content with our own comfort and salvation but to realize that we are living at the time of a great epoch, a great birth, where the transition of the lesser light to the greater is swiftly taking place. Among our young people there are great Souls. I think they are in many ways wiser, deeper, more awake, more enquiring and much more human and full of a deep curiosity which was not so apparent in our earlier time, and because of this sensitivity they are going to react much more violently to our sense of truth, right values and so on, and we must be prepared to accept their criticism of some of our bad old ways and realize that perhaps we are not as good as all that and there may be something in what they have to say.

They are newly from Heaven, they are fresh from the Stars, they are closer to birth. We who have become slightly jaded and somewhat scarred, tattered and bent and our forms are a little pushed around, we are not all quite as fresh or new as we were! But an old battered teapot can make as good a cup of tea as a new one! We must become active warriors in this great life and not pitiful relics dragging about, waiting for death and the undertaker before we take on a new issue. Light is permanent, it is the common denominator between all dimensions, all forces, all creations.

Therefore we must lighten our thoughts, because thoughts and colour and fragrance are very dear and close to one another. In treatment, people can be sweet or sour, this is not necessarily a physical odour but one which registers in another way—a fragrance or otherwise, by which I know whether they are going to benefit from their interview or not. It is not their colours, or the perfume used, or how many baths they have; it is the inner light, the transmutation of the light forces within their soul chemistry. This light appears to be perpetual youth, to be the answer, or solution, to most of our human physical problems. As one old Alchemist once said to me, "How I dream of the day when we can do away with medicine, and just speak the Holy Word and light the Light." You see these are not merely dreams of Heaven, they are reproaches from the past. They are telling us quietly and surely that we have missed an awful lot in human pursuits and we have to retrace our steps sometimes into the old mysteries and teachings, to rediscover the roots from which the human race has sprung. We should question the nourishment that we are taking into our minds or the 'nourishment' we are allowing into our bodies, because the fuel we put into the tank does matter. I know some of you may not agree, but the eating of animals will not make our light any better! Another thing we have to realize is that retaliatory thinking produces a scent that antagonizes. It is like a teacher I knew at school who said, "Some days I can walk into the classroom and it smells sweet and good, and then another day I go into that class and it smells horrible, and I know I'm in for a beastly day." What was the aroma? The aroma was from the parents who quarrelled, the financial problems that the children had been pressurized to, the domestic strife through anxieties, and all the domestic scenes, represented in the classroom in those young lives, and there it was, as he said, a mess, and before he could reach the children, or communicate with them and impart what he had to give, he had to work through this pattern that they had brought with them.

So the pure in heart is purity of light, simplicity of purpose. We must look at this atmosphere of living as a part of the new Age, a recognition of a new sense of subtle values, and utilize them within ourselves in a more practical and natural way, and not have to rely upon the mechanical world to put our troubles right. We can go to the subtle world of cause, of events, the world of guess, of maybe, might-be and the unknown. There is no such thing as an unknown-world, there is no such thing as a mystery. There is only that which is still to be told, still to be revealed and the secret of the Path should always be in the state of awaiting the revealing, that is, waiting to accept something new, to get the anticipation, even of a sentence or a few words put together, a theme on a thought. An idea can fill your whole day, your week, with nourishment, a food, a sustenance and your energy levels will increase because you have increased your area of nourishment. The thing to bear in mind is that you do not increase this merely for yourself but for your community, your family, for those with whom you work. They are the beneficiaries, not so much yourself. It is in the area of your work, the climate of your living and the pattern of your radiations that the work is done. It is done on the invisible plane, yet it is real, deep work.

Fear is the greatest barrier to spiritual worlds and spiritual philosophy. If you do not believe me just think of all the things you have worried about that have never happened. Who has put them right? Has your worry, your fear, your sleepless nights? No! The mystery of the moving event, the great pageant of the unfolding, the revealing, the transmuting, the changing—the Angels in charge of us have done it, and so we can go on into the great realm of transient beauty, of texture, colour, form, shades of such glory and wonder that we are but on the fringe of bringing them into a colour-hungry, Soul-starved, frightened, sick world. If we can bring just that shade closer a new form of reality and communication, then all our self-work, self-revelation, self-discipline, self-giving, will have been invested in the lives of our fellow incarnate Beings, and perhaps, who knows, that is the sole reason for which we have come!

MEDITATION

Now we will enter into meditation, and I want you to feel that this new fragrance and rhythm, this new gentleness and nourishment, this subtle communication, is now establishing itself in you, in your Spirit, in your Etheric Light, and is setting up new waves of activity and forms of creativity as well as inner peace and outer serenity.

CHAPTER TEN

Harmony within Nature

In most occult and esoteric teachings we find there is more than one meaning to an apparently simple statement, with the result that we have to develop the technique of searching deeper for the hidden meaning behind those statements and find within them a sense of depth which is often lacking in everyday conversational meaning. This does not mean that esoteric research calls for double-thinking. It calls for deeper thinking and a more realistic approach to the value of thought, rather than a superficial way of thinking which deals with the everyday routine of life. It is very noticeable in those who begin to study the deeper levels of the mind force that they become more balanced and refined personalities, as if some inward strength is released in their seeking which enters into their relationship with life and people. This seems to release an aura of potential within them—a silent expectation or waiting which is lacking in those who see only the superficial meaning of things. When we speak of the harmony of nature within life, we are dealing with tremendous forces which have their basis in the primitive pattern of evolutionary life and have their origin in many dimensions. Harmony creates a plane of meeting where these forces can mingle to form centres from which the thinking life can operate, and by absorbing a great deal of invisible knowledge or insight, by reaching out into human and spiritual space, we find that the personality enriches itself without any obvious teaching or learning, as if this plateau of living were a state of mental energy where each of us creates in our own way and in our own time.

The product of evolution is the balancing of the forces, that is, the harmonizing of all the polarities and levels of energy which, if they had not this unifying force which brings them together in the universal purpose, would be in a state of continual conflict and disorganization. Instead of that, as we see the evolutionary pattern unfolding, there is a distinct form of unity, a sense of joining together of the extreme parts, finding in the polarities a meeting and a neutrality which is quite amazing and wonderful and yet deeply mysterious. We are not quite sure what this power of the harmonizing neutrality is, but we know that it has a universal role and that its forces and energies are a radiation which extends in and through matter, though having origin in some much higher state. In fact, the balancing of harmony is not only a force within a force, it is more even than that, it is an Intelligence working within the laws; and if we think of the natural laws which govern and make possible an orderly Universe, if we consider the wonderful mathematical calculation and balance whereby all the different cycles, time sequences and movements of the whole systems of the Heavens work in complete unity and harmony, then we realize that this Radiation or Intelligence which unifies these movements, must be vast, profound and deep.

As we witness this harmonizing, unifying force in the outer Universe it is for us as students on the Path to see how and where this applies to the individual, because we are the outer and the inner forms in miniature, therefore, what is in the Universe, seen or unseen, is also within us. The human and spiritual personality has the same potential as its Creator, which means that we have an equal potential to harmonize the various polarities and energies within ourselves and bring them into the same orderliness which is typical of the Universe as a whole.

Now we begin to see that harmony is not a state of inactivity, inertia, nor some kind of drowsiness, but a distinct intelligence, re-organizing and bringing together all the life forces and centralizing them into a productive pattern, projecting itself into the future. This means that we must raise our sights considerably from our restricted frontier of complacency and realize that the members on the Path who are to transmute the dis-harmonizing forces, are themselves often in a state of intense conflict and, in the early stages, will find themselves torn by all kinds of indecisions and temptations and may even know physical and personal torment. This is the Gethsemane by which the human ego passes through the initial stages or periods, gathering his strength, so that eventually he is able to measure it against larger and deeper forces by direct experience. The Bible speaks of this power when it refers to the peace-makers—it says that 'they shall see God!' This is an important point to bear in mind, because in any form of self-development, the centre of a person's Being is their true character. The 'who' or GOD at the centre—is easily discernible because if self is at the centre, that person is always complaining. If GOD is at the centre, then there is a universal sense of making the best of everything. It is as simple as that. This ability to adjust or adapt, to yield, to give, to cede, and to find within these relative influences, not discord, but the skill of a spiritually minded seeker who is able to live within these forces and manifest a deep sense of harmony and poise. Another thing one notices in those who are becoming accustomed to the insight of these various energies, is their capacity to deal with crises. A crisis is really a point or centre at which many, often confusing, issues have arrived at a given point at a certain time. Our ability to cope with, to handle that situation, will be a very great test, almost an Initiation; to take these sets of conflicting circumstances, not be thrown nor confused by them, or, in other words, become discordant. Another noticeable thing is, that people who have developed a spiritual, though not necessarily a religious, philosophy seem able to cope much better with the crises as they emerge than those who have not. It seems that this ability to harness, to equalize, to bring back a sense of proportion, and create a state of harmony is a very powerful personal penetration. So much so, that we can use this same power or force to harmonize the nature forces into obeying this inner sense, this inner radiation, by which the mind personality is able to exert its harmonizing influence, pouring its oil on the troubled waters of the discordant areas of life.

This should teach us that we can do more work by living than by doing, because a person who has this type of aura and radiation will, wherever they go, bring a sense of harmony and peace with them, whether they are aware of it or not. In the therapeutic field we find that the re-establishment of the balanced plateau of harmony within the personality, is the first stage of healing and until that can be firmly re-established and brought into quiet action, the discordant forces will tear that organ to pieces. The discordancies represent illnesses by which the body can be attacked and to which the mind can be subjected and which only the Spirit can overcome. We are beginning to see that harmony, or peace, is not a state of cessation but is one of intense constant activity.

Here we go a little deeper and question the personality of the individual. This is not a question of what we call reality or illusion because most of us prefer illusion to reality! It is an escape from the pressure of responsibility, and, therefore, we are prone to retreat into illusion or part-excuses, rather than face an issue of harmony; we would rather leave a state of discordancy and run away. This conflict of courage is a thing which every Initiate must be prepared to face and we shall have these issues to meet constantly in the course of our development. It is as if our Guardian Ones every now and then give us a run-through to see how really tough and balanced we have become! It is this kind of trial of strength which produces courage, and this is the point.

As many diseases are contagious, that is, they are passed on by contact between people, so is discordancy contagious in the same way; people find themselves pushed into positions of authority and responsibility but because they are discordantly sick at heart, they are restless, agressive, they resent their fellow-men, and the only balm for their Soul is ambition. They often rise to the top of their chosen profession, but they rule a sick empire by their technique of 'hire, fire—sack and destroy.' In other words, they inflict their peculiar tragedy—through the power they have usurped—into the lives of others. Commercial sickness or ambition, whether it be in the political, religious, industrial or economic worlds, is well known. Here we see the individual entering into competition with forces far beyond himself. These people have not the capacity to deal with the forces they attract to themselves, which invariably, is a life with money as the main motive, leading either to sudden death or a long illness. Neither the body nor the mind can stand such a continuous conflict of interposing forces which destroy the even level of that person's living.

Now, as we see this in the larger state, so also is it in the smaller state. It has been said, and there may be some truth in it, that we are our own executioner and tormenter, our own judge, even our own jury, in the fact that this is how we identify ourselves with the various issues of the life in which we are contained, that is, how do we respond to the conflicts which are within us? Here again, it needs self-work. It is no good saying a thing does not exist, because it does exist within us and is all a part of evolution, working out into these power fields, developing individually, collectively, mentally and spiritually, a tremendous power of resources which, in other lives we shall utilize to its greatest extent.

To take this a little further, try to realize that this and other worlds are kept in harmony and balance by very evolved Beings, who are given assignments in various fields, which they are expected to maintain in rhythm, and feed and encourage the cycle of events, harmonize atmospheres and environments and produce conditions whereby lower life can evolve and work under their protection. The same thing applies to us in an ordinary family. The aura, or atmosphere, the parents provide is the 'umbrella', the climate, in which children gather from their parents force, until they are ready to acquire their own. So parenthood is really only an extension of what we call the protective Hierarchy where evolved Beings are given, as assignments, sections of evolutionary forces which become their care, their children and their future. Those words "And the Angels shall have charge over thee lest thy foot be dashed against a stone" are very true in that the evolution of all systems is only by the higher serving the lower; and we in our turn serve our particular lower or higher forces, according to how we feel and live.

Now we go even deeper and begin to turn an enquiring searchlight on what we call the reaction responses of our personal issues. Identification is one of the great problems of human thinking, that is, instead of allowing the wisdom of the event to work out the problem in a natural form and pattern, we quarrel or fight with it and resent it. We even insert our own personality energy into it, with the result that what would have been a minor event—hardly noticeable—becomes a tyrant, an obstacle, a cross so heavy to bear, that we wonder if The Lord has picked us out for some special punishment. The Lord has not done that, I can assure you, it is entirely our own selectivity! We have pushed ourselves right into that situation and become involved in its complexity without having the ability to hold or to understand it; therefore, we are where we should not be—we have rushed in where the Angels would fear to tread and the result is our personality conflicts become long, miserable, sad or hopeless. Now this does not mean that we should avoid life participation but that we seek in another way, without conflict—and this is difficult because most of us are trying to do each other some good—to convert somebody, sell them our ideas, push our literature into their hands or to give them some good advice—in other words, interference seems to be a form of social, biological urge.

This, again, is interference with the balance of harmony within the forces of those people's lives. What we have to offer, they may have finished with or are not ready for. Non-interference is a more or less sacred teaching. In most of the Eastern religions this sense of non-interference goes too far sometimes, in that if one meets a situation of real Karmic debt, some walk on the other side of the road, shrug their shoulders and say, "It's nothing to do with us. It is your Karma." Well, that is just too easy! We cannot completely evade the issue but we certainly must not interfere.

This is where discipline and self-observation is so urgently needed; when these situations turn up, realize that this is the centre of forces which are flowing in all directions. To get caught in them, is to be torn. But learn to swim with them, live and float with them, be a friend within them instead of an enemy, in a very short time, the situation completely reverses and what was an enemy becomes a friend—what before was against becomes to your benefit, because the evolutionary process is to make everything better—it is to evolve, to progress, to improve. We seem to think that the Lords of Creation cannot do this unless we stick our finger into the human pie, stir it up, insert our ignorance and imagine we can do the job much better.

Now this means that we must think about what we say and do to people. One of the cheapest forms of entertainment is giving advice! Fortunately, patent medicines are getting dearer now but at the time when they were cheaper people used to buy them by the dozen to send to their friends! Look into the medicine chest or into the bathroom cupboard. See the different forms of retreat, excuses or evasions we have tried to cure by chemical means when actually it was a mental conflict —it will be quite surprising! In fact, few people throw their remedies away. We keep them as a loving keepsake 'just in case', even when the label is completely gone! Now what is it that makes us cling to something which is not essentially real? There is a difference between a person who is real and one who is imitating. There is a distinct aura about a person who has really worked within their personality and has developed a silent strength and wisdom. If we must collect, let it be with a discerning mind, almost as if we have a lovely rose garden and we do not want everybody depositing their junk, their waste material, their patent medicines, their bad advice into it. It needs strength to hold one's peace, because in doing so one is holding harmony. Many people want advice. They go round getting it from all their friends as a form of entertainment, and when they have it all, they still do exactly what they meant to do in the first place! But they have meantime absorbed a lot of time and sympathy, and to give these unduly is not wise.

So bear in mind that in harmony there is not only the personality and mental forces at work, but the psycho-forces also, and this takes us on to the astral plane. As we develop a spiritual philosophy, mental stability increases; conversely, lack of spiritual knowledge seems to weaken the mental resistances. A good rich working philosophy strengthens, and this is very necessary when dealing with the astral field.

We all need fuel, that is insight, inspiration and teaching. These harmonizing influences come fourth-dimensionally from which they flow into a third-dimensional plane. We are now putting the first principle to work, we are reaching in and working with our thought forces into the higher dimension and drawing from there the resources of the forces of balance, rather than the chaos, confusion, discordancy and the lower orders of the third dimension, trying or expecting to find food, nourishment and balance in the lower dimension to which we belong, to which we must continually reach out.

I mentioned the word astral. There are certain states of sensitivity where we touch areas of thought forms which are not of this earth—and they are certainly not of Heaven. It is this intermediate world of illusion, the psyche-world, which perhaps offers man his greatest stumbling block to reaching into the truly harmonious spheres. The psyche is the first stage of the astral where people pass immediately after physical death—but that does not mean that they become perfect! Death is not the solution to problems, and self-destruction is not a way out, for the confusion of the people who take this way is sometimes great and their remorse, on the in-between planes, can be terrible. This plane can affect certain people whose harmonic structures are not very sure, and for this reason we find that certain depressions, influences, fears and anxieties are astral in some sense, that they may have origin, not in an earth-mind but in the astral, the 'in-between' state in which the mind force feels or registers such disturbances. In a psychic condition, such as a haunted house, where linger the thought-forces of some violent scene which has been enacted, walk into that house even years afterwards, this influence will remain. This is the influence of earthbound Souls who in remorse, tragedy and sorrow, are immersed in its unforgiveness. The Spiritual forces can always overcome and reach through these planes of shadows, but there are those who are not mentally enriched, not strong enough, who sometimes become influenced by these lesser forces. Here is where the Spiritually-minded person is so important, because by the deepening and strengthening of Spiritual resources, these people can be helped enormously, by presence, by Spiritual security within self, by thought, prayer, even by just being, one can be a great source of strength to these and other people. Bringing eventually these lost ones through their shadows and valleys. Thus through strength, harmony and courage, one becomes a saviour in a certain way, a healer or comforter to those whose mental ability is much more shallow, less strong, and who are in need of someone who is on the Path, whose strength and insight is sufficient to help and lift them into the enjoyment of a new harmonic world.

So you see, it is a great benefit to get enough people to understand the balance of harmony and its value, who are ready to sacrifice some of their convenience, use a little self-discipline to stop their bad temper and quick tongues, to cease criticism and poor advice, who do not pass judgment on their fellow human beings, or condemn them behind their backs. So many can only talk of morbidness and sex; can only see the mortality, the tragedy of the human family, and because there is a greater proportion of this type of thinking to the proportion of those who are awakened, who are stimulated to the new urgency of the new world, the New Age worker must become involved in balancing and developing these resources within his own nature, because it is not only important to raise the consciousness of the individual but to raise the whole plane of thought-forces to act as a great peacemaking, harmonic unity, a great flow-force which can maintain peace in a chaotic world so that the tragedy of wars can cease. Wars are made by mental attitudes, by allowing the discordant forces of the lower and external worlds to find a lodgment in the tragedy of human ambition, so sacrificing ones fellow man to the systems of its judgment. That kind of price need not be paid, provided we have enough people who begin to become aware of harmony centres within themselves, by which the personality, the home, the vicinity, the district, the nation, the world itself can be brought into a tremendous harmonic flow of unity of purpose, instead of discordancy and war, the temptation to use force instead of harmony. No doubt this is one of the great periods by which mankind and the personality of the Soul has been tested because we participate here at a very homely level yet achieve a tremendous universal force. The Bible* again refers to this when it says that a certain city was saved because of ten just men. It was not that they were 'just' in the sense of being just, but they were 'aware', they were living Spiritual Beings who were not immersed in religious dogma or in the rights of religion. They were in a sense universal people, who were sharing and participating in world events by their living, thinking and doing. In their quiet silence, the alliances of their harmonious disciplines were able to bring peace instead of destruction to a city and save it.

We have already had two world wars in living memory; there is a great need now for all the esoteric and deep-teaching schools to realize that they have other work to do besides the question of self-evolution. This is the extending of ourselves into the Universal concept, not only for ourselves, but for our present environment, providing that material by which the New Age world of unity, the brotherhood of nations and the divine principle can happen much more quickly because people have been prepared to listen, to learn, to wait and to dig deeply into their own potential and release there this great wealth, this power, which can calm the troubled seas and ease the harrassed atmosphere—can bring the voice of comfort and strength into the torment and the sorrow.

* Genesis 19, 23–33.

115

This is self-work which can last us all our lives, but bear in mind that the health pattern and mental conflicts go together. The life we want to live, the universal world servers we would aim to be, can only be made fully possible by developing the power of inward harmony, by non-identification, by a great compassion, a great mercy, but non-interference.

Let the wisdom of the evolving event participate within, do not get into crises, think that the end of the world is coming, starvation, growing old or some malignant disease—throw all that stuff out because it is third-dimensional material which belongs entirely to the primitive state. We have no use for it. We are entering now into fourth-dimensional communication, where the higher forces are blending deeply and richly into human affairs, into human conduct. Therefore, every school which teaches the evolving life principle as a part of its plan and contribution, is important.

A great strain, perhaps, but a real necessity, is placed upon us, on all of us, to maintain this inward and outward force of control, discipline and contribution, because it is not only our own lives that are involved, it is the lives of the unborn, the waiting Souls who are ready to enter this Earth. Because we have lived it may be better, it may be worse, it is for our own consciousness to answer that problem with a deep sense of purpose. Begin this thing, radically and consciously now. Remember that discords and disharmonies are not of the higher dimensions, they belong only to our lower dimensional form. If we can disentangle and separate ourselves from the lower conflicts, ignore them and get on with the work of self-living, raising the consciousness above the body itself, above the mind, we can utilize this great universal power, that it not only heals, not only blesses, but makes possible the birth of new worlds. Take all things within yourselves, harmonize them and send them out again, so that you become a barometer, a plateau of safety, security, sanity and good balance; so that the world can be enriched by your work and we in our turn can all share more deeply in the evolutionary mystery in which we are permanently involved.

MEDITATION

So, now as we enter silence, surrender every fear, relax yourselves—undo your knees, undo your tight hands, loosen your furrowed brows, let your shoulders go, and from this minute, surrender all tensions, all fears, all conflicts— reach out into this higher dimensional nourishment where true food for thought, inspiration, guidance and love pour forth healing into the life-force—do this consciously, deeply and with feeling.

CHAPTER ELEVEN

Unity—Cosmos and Chaos

Unity is a word which has been used very loosely in the development of the idea by which harmony or the resolution of discords can be achieved, but we now see this word and the principle of unity in an entirely different light. We must visualize this as the blending of the life principle and forces—that is, the equalizing or the balancing of the inner self with qualities of our primitive nature and coming to terms with our spiritual self. In other words, unity is not just a state of peace, it is a state of activity with continual reaching out into new fields of energy to unify and draw these energies into the personality focus. This is very important because we cannot expect to live safely in a private static world. We are in the mainstream of the evolving principle which is carrying us along through Time, continually exposing us to new hazards of living, new horizons and new forces. It is the adaptation of the life force which seems to have made possible the evolutionary selection; to be able to accept and utilize to any stress or tension seems to have been the nature principle by which man has survived. This power of adaptation is also a mental force in the fact that the thought world will decide what is unity or disunity. It is this pre-conditioning of the adapting principle, at which those who are studying esoteric knowledge, must begin to take a new look, because here we have the answer to most mental illnesses and perhaps to many of the physical problems which overcome the human nature and cause it to become victimized by the forces in which it is involved.

We find that within his psycho-nature man has not emerged very far from his first state of civilization, or taken many steps

118

beyond his primitive survival patterns. In fact, we can say that mankind is only just emerging into a civilized state and as yet has not come to terms with his primitive background in proportion to the future of this civilization. Now, to adapt from the primitive to the cultural system of today has incurred a tremendous amount of experiment, and much of it disastrous, for the simple reason that we cannot expect to deal with the colossal forces of the Solar and Cosmic worlds while being in total ignorance of them.

In the deepening of our nature we come to the realization that the elements are not only capable of being extended but they also have another dimensional foothold—not just for three dimensional resolution.

To explain this further—if we have no knowledge of continuity, and no idea of future worlds or pre-existence, if we are completely ignorant of the purpose of life, then our method or route of adaptation is very small. This means that this extensive pre-knowledge by which the life forces are recognized, if not known, cannot prepare the mental or spiritual nature to adapt itself to stress, to exposure, to the hazard of living, while at the same time promoting a tremendous rate of growth in the mental-psycho field.

Before we go further into the balance of unity we must first analyse what we call the psycho mechanisms. These we recognize as a form of insurance which man has built up by various religions, by pagan worship and by systems which assure him against the unknown. The unknown, as you will agree, has been man's greatest fear, and, therefore he tries to placate these forces —hence his deep superstition.

In a recent debate on primitive superstition, the theory was put forward—and this has some bearing on what we are discussing—that superstition and gambling go together—that the more superstitious the nature of the person the deeper is the inclination to gamble, to dice against the unknown future. Thus where perhaps a third of the nation's turnover of monetary values is linked to gambling, we can see that man has not moved very far from his superstitious background—that superstitions are still working in his nature; hence, he tries to find some stimulus or security against the unknown factor of death.

Now, we must go further, and realize that we cannot replace one system by another unless it has some mental advantage. We need to pass from the field of superstition and enter the field of the known value. This is where occult science and ancient wisdom can come into its own; it has been lost on the way, suppressed by the various systems wherein man's individuality was denied him, except he worship through a particular method. Individual worship, individual evolution, was not a thing encouraged in the mass with the result that rebels were very harshly dealt with and those who had any reason to doubt the so-called authority of the system were quickly brought to heel, and persecution,* religious and otherwise, besprinkles our history with many sordid pages. Where man is trying to reach outside the fixed system of evolution and enter the freedom of his mind and mental conduct, he is stepping out on his personal responsibility, using his mind, his Soul, his Spirit for direct communication with the Force that he knows as GOD.

This, at first, sounds rather complicated, but is not if we trace the steps by which man is rediscovering his heritage. It was there once, it has been lost, and here we have the opportunity of bringing it back again through these various systems of conflict, but where we shall see them as a part of the work—that chaos, not peace, is really the builder. We have the example of two dynamic principles working, one is the principle of creativity and the other is of decay, and the principle of decay is just as important as that of creativity. At this stage, it is necessary that chaos or decay must have its own fertilizing—the breaking-down of the past, of old systems, old ideas and even of old bodies—thus it is removing continually the residual poisons of civilization and of man's thinking, living and doing. In fact, decay is really a great cleansing and preparing of the soil for the future.

We will go yet deeper into the question, because we find that

* 'The Cathars', Arthur Guirdham.

the life-force principle is impregnated into the bloodstream, therefore, the bloodstream becomes the focal point by which the life-principle element flows throughout the entire bodyforce. Once we can concede this as an actual element which flows in and out through the various creative aspects, we can begin to discern another facet of truth which has escaped us. This question of the blood, that is, the life force or the life principle contained within it, is also linked with the principle of decay. As the life force withdraws from the bloodstream, decay immediately sets in, so the balance of the vitality of creativity in our bodies is in the bloodstream; as it decreases so does decay increase; as it intensifies, decay lessens. So corruption or corrosion is really an occult explanation by which the substance of change is manifested. We know in our therapeutic work that the bloodstream is important from the physical and chemical viewpoint, as well as from the spiritual aspect, and those who have impure bloodstreams find it very difficult to maintain a spiritual content. The purer we can form the pattern by right diet, right thinking and natural balanced action, the more vital the bloodstream becomes, the creative principle is more active, the decaying principle lessened.

Now we begin to see chaos and unity, working as partners, not as enemies. The one is removing worn, decayed tissues, the other is building new life to replace that which has been removed. Here we see that all illness is not bad, that decay is not all putrid, that whatever ferments is not necessarily bad, that what is in a state of change is not necessarily unhealthy. This we recognize at the level to which we have attained at this minute. Let us discuss in more detail this question of how chaos is unified into the character. Again, we turn to ancient occultism to find a relative explanation of this in the Law of Opposites.* Chaos exists to break down the primitive substance prior to its change into a higher substance, that is the Law of Transmutation.† But here we go into character and nature and climate of individuality, and find we all have a destructive part in our nature and mind.

*† Yoga of the Inward Path.

We are all very close to chaos perhaps closer than we are to unity, in that it is easier to destroy, to denounce, to criticize and judge, to be ungrateful, thankless and complaining—in fact, all those elements of what we call the lesser virtues are really elements of chaos. Anger, hasty judgment, all the things we are not very proud of, are a part of the chaotic elements working in conflict. So here we have the battle right on our doorstep. We ourselves are unity and conflict, chaos and creativity, working within our character and nature, as we learn, live, act, and balance ourselves, so are we an arena of this personal evolutionary aspect, each one of us experimenting in our own particular way. We may find one day that the delinquencies of youth, the desperate need to destroy or injure, may have as its cause something different from what we have hitherto thought. It may be a deep spiritual resentment, against the platitudes, the fixed society into which it has been born; it has nothing much to replace it because it has not yet earned wisdom or merit but it is closely allied to the chaotic principle, the principle which resents decay.

So before we denounce our youngsters because they are resisting the fixed pattern imposed upon them, let us go further into the cause and effect and ask if we are giving them the opportunity to create the world which they have come to build? —or are we causing resistance to be such that the chaotic forces within them erupt into this tempest which we see throughout the entire world? That we must leave for future historians and the science of spiritual understanding—that is, the birth of science in the human Soul—to other generations.

In the next part of this chaos/unity we find another pattern, which we know as transmutation. We are all continuously transmuting, converting one thing into another. We are changing our chemistry, exchanging oxygen and hydrogen, changing the various fuels and foods; we are transmuting darkness into light, from the moment we first breathe to the moment we cease —converting the elements of the forces of nature within ourselves, known and unknown.* The law of transmutation is not

* Yoga of the Inward Path.

a new thing, but we can take it to another level so that from the digestive or decay system, we can elevate it to the mental-psycho level. Now the difference here is that the Initiate on the Path does not seek merely to transmute but also to learn to manifest, for the difference between mere words and the actual power to transmute, is the ability to manifest.

We have talked of laws of decay and laws of creativity; we spoke of the law of opposites, and so on, and there are many others, but we must ask ourselves, can we manifest these laws? The answer is that we should be able to do so, to a very great extent; we are not as helpless as we think we are, and the positive force to change, to transmit and even transmute body cells is beginning to be accepted as a natural part of another system of medicine; the ability to change cell-life, to change the condition of the blood, to change the whole rhythm of the life force can be made to manifest. The difference here is that one system is teaching and the other is manifesting. Our system, the one we are dealing with at the moment, is manifestation. Esoteric teachings such as this have always been attached to a Therapeutic school, so that its teachings can be made manifest, where other teachings are just hope, maybe's and might-be's. In other words, the esoteric student becomes a working partner within these manifested laws and not just an onlooker. We do not have to go back two thousand years to substantiate the natural laws of balance and living. We know, by direct experience, that these things are applicable here and now, just as much—perhaps even more so, with our educated though destructive minds—than they were with the superstitious thought of the very early Jewish era.

Now, we need a tremendous amount of courage to step out of this stage of part-knowing into the stage of recognition and full knowledge. It is almost a passing from the world of the possible to the impossible, from the world of the non-miracle to that of the miracle where we can emerge from visualizing a world immersed in suffering to such an extent that it is helpless and hopeless, into a vitality of thinking where the Spirit is able to change those various systems and conditions very quickly and radically by the power to manifest. Most of you have seen these various methods of occult science manifested in our particular way, in diagnosis, in prognosis, in the different radiations, thought-form pictures and other means of natural communication.

Here we are moving from the age of teaching or preaching to the age of manifesting; that is, we no longer need be continual victims of chaos. We have this tremendous ability to establish the unity of these laws and forces and bring them within the nature and character, into a definite mechanism, the means by which we can change and raise the consciousness of these various elements with which we have been born.

Let us return again, for a moment, to this question of the bloodstream. We have in the Christian teaching a re-birth of this idea that the blood is the vitality of the Spirit. Unfortunately their teaching of personal sacrifice and the 'atonement' on the Cross is a kind of 'follow-on' from the ancient concept of animal sacrifices—symbolized by the lamb—but let us look at it from a chemical-spiritual point of view. If we lose our temper, our blood pressure increases. Extreme tension can cause thrombosis, coronaries and other forms of blood pressure temperature diseases. Congestions form through the active emotional mind-force involved in the body—in other words, we can kill the life-force principle by anger, hate, resentment, or fear. The fact that we can bend or divert this life-force principle within the chemistry of the body by applied forces of nature and character, brings us rather close to this factor, we are our own doctors, our own physicians, or surgeons, in the respect that what is happening within the body chemistry is either unity with the life-force principle within the bloodstream, or it is a constant contradiction and feeding of the decay forces within the body system, according to character, mood and intellect.

This is the strange thing. Many people seem to live good lives and yet nothing seems to happen for them. I was once speaking to a very prominent churchman who was most indignant that ordinary people such as we should be able to manifest while he, being a member of his system, particularly blessed and full of authority, could not do this thing! He thought that GOD was very unjust and the whole thing was quite wrong and certainly did not match up with his ideas of Divine Justice. This force is not a question of merit. It is a question of capacity. Get hold of that and one can begin to see doors and corridors opening up—as capacity, and it is here where this kind of work helps, that is, by self-work, self-revelation, by direct experiences, one can build up the capacity to receive these communications and forces from a plane on a higher level, not because we are good or are any better than others, but because through self-work of discovery we have developed the capacity to receive. This is slow at first. Many people are not aware when they start to receive, when the capacity was beginning to enlarge itself. All we know is that it is very difficult now to live and deal with people whose capacity is still shut down, who do not feel and speak in the extended sense of living, who have not eyes to see nor ears to hear, who are shut in to their material, physical, superstitious selves and have not sought to enlarge their life-force, their work, their temperament, their character, by reaching out to the higher, rarefied, purified elements and remanifesting them, drawing them into their life-force, into their mental and spiritual thinking; in fact, as capacity increases, the gulf between oneself and those who are still asleep can become so wide that it is very difficult to go back into those elements of mental and physical darkness and be compatible with them. This, perhaps, is one of the tests of those who are seeking on the Path, the enlightenment of the Soul, but at this stage none would like to go back, to revert to that state of 'stomach, money, bed'—and nothing else! We would not like to think that we were isolated from this delightful sense of evolution, the participating principle, the new awareness of the elements and forces involved in life; to be shut off from this would be to be thrown back into darkness.

So capacity—the capacity to receive, and to transmit, is really the barometer by which this form of work and revelation, becomes individual, personal and intimate between self and

GOD, the Universe and life in general. It is a personal relationship, with no systems in between, no one to say do this or do that, for we are not responding to the Divine Source. The purpose of free will is to enable this capacity to develop, to give us freedom of our own mental gymnastics, of spiritual and psycho reaching-out. Free-will is the doorway to the capacity to receive; provided it is used and applied in the sense for which it was intended, though it may be difficult to understand that chaos is necessary.

We must conclude with the necessity to unify, that is, to bring into unity these inter-play forces within character or nature, within atmosphere and climate, and not control but transmute them, because controlling does not solve the problem, so that eventually, these forces within our nature pass from the conflict of control into the unity of transformation. There now no longer has to be a constant war between the various nature levels for they become involved in the deeper unity of the first state of consciousness, the life principle working. This, I think, was what the Christ was trying to make us understand in the words that Truth would set us free, that life was to be more abundant, that decay, sorrow and death should cease. This was demonstrated in the non-decay of His body, where transmutation was able to take over from the force of chaos or decay and the body force was able to dissolve its essence into the finer ethers without passing through the chaos, the shadows and valleys of conflict.

This then is our work. By observation of self by self—for nobody can observe better than we because we are always with ourself! Thus, when we find conflict or chaos come tumbling out of our nature and character by thought, word, deed, just watch them—stand aside, listen to self talking, watch self acting, study self preaching and look at self acting all over again. Now once we can achieve this the spiritual psycho force—which is anyhow separate from the body—only very lightly joined at birth and will very quickly dissolve itself at termination—we can use this awareness of the body, physical-life-nature, reacting and living its part. Observation is the cure. Once we

126

know of, or are aware of a thing, we are three parts towards being able to transmute it. Unless we are aware, we have not the blueprint, the pattern, or example. Self-observation brings self-awareness. Self-awareness brings selflessness. This produces courage, and courage produces services, and service produces freedom.

When again we think of unity and chaos, and of various platitudes, of so-called peace and so on, remember the Path and the Way is direct experience from the earliest part of earth-life right up to its termination; every moment is an enrichment and increases the capacity, enlarges the potential and makes that life-force in itself a power-house of direction, transmutation and creativity.

This is our vision, this is our future. Now let us begin our work.

MEDITATION

Here let us sit for a few moments, and in the Silence feel that your Quest is on and that you have started to reach out to the great power-house of existent forces, feeling yourself a living part of the creative principle.

CHAPTER TWELVE

The Quest

In the quest for these principles try to understand that a state of union is the innermost hunger of every Soul in its search for its own Pathway. Each individual Pathway is influenced by the birth-Ray, of only that one, and alongside this is the great Karmic Path which is unfolding itself within the personality. We are, as we have said the past history of the Planet. We are also its future and its true creative force through which the GOD-Principle can manifest. Thus the existence of a GOD-Principle is manifest through human Souls living in human bodies, and the descent of the Spirit into lower dimensions is the means by which evolution takes place; this is the true death, this the sacrifice by which the Soul renounces much of its treasure, its accumulated knowledge and powers, and surrenders itself to a discipline in lower dimensional birth whereby it may participate in the lower creative forces, thus unifying itself more deeply with the creative principle of Life.

This can be very difficult because then the personality becomes involved in these forces and elements and is often victimized by them and the very Spirit itself can thus be degraded.

We also find that this primitive life-force dictates to the Soul-force, causing confusion and feelings of guilt. The Soul at this time is not able to draw fully upon its real resources, and sickness of the physical body often appears; this is due mostly to lack of nourishment of the Soul-force, and as we enter deeper into the lower dimensions the sense of hunger increases. This becomes greatest when we are furthest from our power source.

Sometimes it seems that the Quest leaves us suspended in space, and at this time of our greatest need we find ourselves at the moment of greatest weakness. It is during this exposure of the personality to the conflict of the elements and of the whole past, that many people fail within their life, and retreat from it, and seek to escape to a state of sleep.

This state of division—of density—is so acute in many cases that it is in itself a mental illness, indeed many of our so-called illnesses are really undernourishments where demands of life are out of proportion to the needs—that is, the hunger is greater than the food available. At first we find that we can satisfy the ordinary human quest by physical appetites. We can become so busy with these that the Soul-Quest can be suppressed and submerged, but there comes a time in every person's life when the Quest of the Soul comes so close to the surface mind that it forces itself into every issue upon which the personality is engaged.

If you want evidence of this, trace back incidences in your own life, some noticeable, many not, which have brought you to this present moment. The books you read, the discussions with people you met, the persuasion of your conscience, the unrest of your Soul, and you will trace, incident by incident, where slowly and surely the Soul-pressures have brought you to a state of recognition. Much of this evolution is termed compulsion through hunger. We are quite accustomed to having to work to eat, which is a form of instinctive compulsion, and many other forms by which we subscribe to the natural power-forces to exist, but there comes a time when we evolve not by compulsion, but because we want to. This is a very important part of life, for it is the moment when we cross the bridge between the dimensions into the mystery of our future. You cannot be sure when or how it happened, and if anyone asks you to give reasons and facts or to explain to them why it is you feel and think and live as you do, it would be difficult for you to give a logical, reasoned answer.

But what we are concerned with now is that the Quest has started and the Soul-hunger reaches out and becomes even more acute. Many people who take up Esoteric studies complain that once they become awakened their sense of responsibility quickens. This should be fully understood because a Soul, before awakening, has possibly wasted half of its lifetime sequence and, therefore, in the other half, it has to pack in a tremendous assignment of self-work to fulfil the purpose of coming. So it really means that at the time we think we are growing old and so should take life more easily, mentally and esoterically, we find that a new pressure, a new rhythm, a new urgency, a new need begins to take over, and has a revitalizing effect upon our mental and spiritual activity.

The next thing to realize is that the strain may be very heavy at first as we are exposed to rapid experience—as a philosopher once put it: "The awkward Soul lives seven days in one."

If we go a little deeper, we shall find that the various hungers and needs of individuals are locked within a secret chamber which the occultists of old used to call 'The unknown treasure of the heart.' By this it was reasoned that as no one really knew what was in the heart or of its hungers, it had to be exposed to love and hate, to anger and heat, to light and cold until it became tempered in the fires of love's exposure. Many people complain that GOD has a way of running HIS world all wrong! People die at the wrong time, troubles come when they are not wanted, problems arise out of blue skies and instead of living a life of tranquil bliss, they often find they are living a very active life of mental change and challenge! This is the difference between a state of sleep and a state of awareness.

Now here we must go even deeper into what we call the desire forces of each life. Some of these desires are so negative that, quite frankly, we are ashamed and never speak of them. This is a pity because so much of our desire force is good, but, because it has a sense of shame or guilt or impossibility attached to it, it is seldom utilized except by the poets, the artists and visionaries, and those who are not afraid of guilt or of appearing to be different. It is in this sense of imprisoned shame that we can see the potential of a great Celestial burning of

130

the inward force, at the moment when the Quest comes right to the surface of the mind, and flavours our thinking, our living, our eating, our sleeping and keeps us in a constant state of watchfulness. From this time on it never really leaves us, even through the periods of intense remorse, of looking backwards which can result, of Karma undertaken which was never recognized before.

Now, at this point, I want you to see Karma as three things —the assignment of the individual essence—the individual at birth—the individual Karma of past lives—the world or Planetary Karma in which we share in the manifested path of history. Each one of these three levels is, in a way, a responsibility to us and each must be served in proportion; and thus we climb up first through the personal Karma into the group Karma and then into world service . . . and this is where 'The Quest' comes into its finest hour, because where before we have been personal seekers on a personal quest, we now enter into world service concepts where the promise of the New Age with its work of personal involvement takes away any isolation and from now on completely immerses the new Initiate into its mysterious shape, colours and meaning, often moulding a new character and temperament, and revealing an entirely new nature.

This ability to change our character, nature, outlook and personality is most important, for now the Quest works as yeast within the mould, the hidden splendours and the hidden shames all combine together, and bring forth the blooms, the potentials of people, achievement, understanding and depths of character which before have lain dormant and unrevealed.

It is not easy to take on power to manifest, because power means responsibility. There are many people who would like to heal the world, but I can assure you that if we attempted to heal it or put its problems right, we would be disliked, feared, resented and ridiculed. To think that we have only good wishes towards the world and yet those very wishes can cause us suffering and pain, may be rather a surprise to us in this century, but if we study comparative religions we find that pain and suffering have always been the outcome for the pioneers proclaiming the Spirit of Truth.

We are not asked to be pilloried or sacrificed but we are asked to make sacrifices in another way, and this is the issue. Many want Heaven and Earth at the same time. Most want the peace, the power, the glory of Heaven while still enjoying material possessions, social deceit and 'satisfactions'. It is not wrong that we strive to have the necessities of third-dimensional living but the point is that we cannot serve the Quest for the Holy Grail, and material possessions and power at the same time. It is not so much the small possessions of the individual, as the greater obsession of ideas. Are these inflicted or imposed by various means under the guise of doing good? Some people 'do good' so unwisely that they create discord and wear out the goodwill of all their friends; their good intentions become so intense that everybody dodges round the corner as soon as they appear! In fact, in modern times, 'do good' has become almost an unpleasant word. To try to alter the world to our own ideas or for us to alter ours to the world, that is the issue—and it needs a tremendous discipline on our part to accept these things which may not be in accordance with our feelings and ideas.

To understand this in a simple way, go back to your early hungers and desires and when you compare them with present ideals you find there is a gulf between them. Twenty or so years ago, what you desired, what you wished and hoped for, is completely and entirely different from what you hope and wish for today. Values have been in constant state of eruption, the pressures of evolution, the exchanges of the life-forces, the exposure to experiences, have gradually eroded away many of the primitive forces within us, refining, purifying, strengthening; but this again needs courage to accept.

To be refined, to be strengthened, to be prepared, means exposure to experience, but invariably we resent the experience because it is teaching us something. We have to resist certain things, or to accept certain conditions, and be prepared to change those conditions and not to fight them all the way. Put in a simple way, we have to take GOD on HIS terms and not expect benefits from a GOD-Being to fit our individual requirements. The difference between the personal quest and the Universal Quest is always the problem to the awakening mind.

Now, let us go back a little because here we find that the Quest has certain community forces attached to it which we know as group feeding or nourishment, group encouragement. In the field of medicine, and especially in mental illness, doctors are beginning to find that group nourishment is a very powerful factor in helping to restore a state of balance. To the Initiate on the Path, it is most essential that a group is found within which to find and share a source of nourishment because a Quest without a continual sense of supply is unrewarding. It is almost like going up many culs-de-sac or getting lost on one of these new building estates and being unable to find the way out because it all looks the same. There is a great power manifested within the communal force. So great is this power that outside of it one really feels naked, but within that community is a sense of belonging, of being in a constant state of union.

Another thing we find with work of this nature is that by self-work, self-revelation, by self-discovery, the whole group gets the benefit of each individual's efforts. These go into what may be termed a communal pool and from this all can draw and give, but the thing is, to give more and to draw less. At first, we draw a great deal and give very little because it does not occur to us that we are entitled to give. We have been born into the world, our parents nourish us with food, somebody finds us a job, someone supplies us with money, so we become dependent and instead of being a self-creative pool of energy and resourcefulness, we live far too much off the resources of other people. This again is a state of hunger and of need. For a while it is quite right that we should draw from the pool and receive nourishment, but there comes a time upon this Quest when each Soul must stand within its own right and its own crossroad and decide whether it is going to live a life of giving or a life of taking and, make no mistake about it, we are taught, encouraged, trained and educated to take, take, take. Once we realize that material philosophy is against the Quest philosophy, we can realize what sort of battle we have on our hands. If there is any decision between visible or spiritual comfort, it is practically certain the choice will come down on physical comfort first and spiritual comfort second. It is not until we reach the end and have exhausted our spiritual credit that we begin to find that we are not able to draw upon these resources, that we have, in other words, overdrawn our spiritual bank and we are running on the credit of other people, on their bounty, their charity and generosity, their service and giving; this is a moment of a new revealing. It is also a time which most people dislike. When the Christ said, "Give up all and follow Me," He did not necessarily mean that His disciples should give up all material possessions, but to detach themselves from the power which held them to those possessions, for it is this power which holds us down, which imprisons and enslaves us in this lower communal life instead of engaging our activities in the higher communal life.

There are those words recorded of the two Church dignitaries who were watching a very important and impressive ceremonial procession through Rome with all its glitter and show. Amidst the pomp and the ceremony one turned to the other and said, "We can't say now 'Gold and silver have we none'" and the other said, "Neither can we say 'Take up thy bed and walk'!"

This symbolizes the issue. To be able to manifest into the world of other people's hungers, and their needs, to find the means within our own capacity to feed another's distress; to find in our sorrow the courage to console and comfort; and in our own loss and tragedy a sense of example in which we can give to the world not of our misery but of our depths, our own findings. At that moment, perhaps, when we have lost most, is the time we have most to give.

One might ask, "What is the answer to giving?" It is not necessarily a question of always giving money; it is one of giving in thought, in ideas, in rendering our service not as work but as an assignment, no matter whether we work in a dairy, a shop or a factory. It is not work for an employer, it is personal contribution to world service. It is not how much paper we get in an envelope, it is what we have given in thought to that job, wanted or unwanted, worthy or unworthy; it is the people we meet, the decisions we make, the smiles given, the aches in our hearts we have kept hidden, the courage and the discipline we have been able to use. That is the assignment, not the wage packet, not the individual work but the all-over contribution, our particular Quest, our own giving. To do this, year in and year out and make every part of occupation and work a part of our birth assignment, will make the body ache, and the mind reel, the pockets may be empty and everything around seem quite out of proportion to what we are doing. Some argue and say, "Well, I am doing this for God, I am doing this for someone else, why cannot I get a little more benefit out of it?" and if we are not very careful we will start bargaining with the Almighty, because we are doing a few paltry things and think we are not getting enough reward! It is so easy on the one hand to be magnificent and on the other to be mean.

When meeting real people, perhaps in a therapeutic sense, this can be seen, with a sharpness not possibly seen in other fields. We see a person who is really trying to do their best; there is something big and good and strong in them and we can help those, because of that deep inward strength. Their weakness is their strength, their very needs and hunger—their bigness. The depth of character, the breadth of nature, the deepness of their giving, makes one feel it a homage to help them and to share with them their particular hunger, and their need. When Christ said He would send to the Disciples a Comforter that they no longer should mourn, nor weep, nor be in sorrow, He was referring to the Holy Spirit made manifest in the giving ones. We are that comforter! That world assignment to the New Age is our job, our work, our thinking. So each little crumb of personal honesty, each contribution, unsung, unknown, unrewarded, that is our real work. That is the true Quest.

It is very easy to pray in the market place and be charitable that all men may see, but this is not true work. It is nothing else but bad acting, wrong taking and poor giving. When a person is really seeking one can see this change of personality and character gradually taking shape. There is a sense of depth and a new form of meaning—the face and eyes alter and they think, live and act differently. There is a certain subtle something that shines around them, that seems to manifest from them. Not great perhaps, but powerful none the less.

It is a poor workman who finds fault with his tools, and it is a good workman who can do a good job with poor tools. And we find that we have the potential and the ability, each one of us, to do some simple task, to make a dress, to polish a pair of shoes, to do the hair—not for posterity, but for sheer creativeness, to manifest such that the world is that much more beautiful because we have cast some flower seeds on a waste field— smiled at somebody when the heart was full of misery—plucked up courage to speak, to do, to go—used discipline when everything around said, 'Let go!'—had, in the quietness of the hour, a personal triumph. That is the true Quest.

An interesting question to ask ourselves, is if we would like our son, or daughter to be a Messiah, a Comforter with a world mission, a world Server with no reward, no merit, no title, no anything, would we be happy about that?—only if we were big enough to suffer their reviling with them. 'Well— what are the returns going to be?' Those are the tragic questions asked and those who seek to do things for what they are going to get, or expect to get out of it, are doomed to failure, spiritually speaking, from the start. When things are not running smoothly, people often say to me, 'This should not happen to you; why, when you are helping others, should this be?' This always troubles me because they do not understand the idea of a Quest. It *should* happen to us more than to anybody else, because we should have more exposure, more responsibility, more depth, more demands—not less.

The spiritual nature can only be enriched and strengthened

by these demands, for, faced rightly, they are building up within the innermost nature tremendous resources which many people can make use of. One becomes a spiritual bank, where the poverty and need of other people can be met, and that is rarely a question of money; it is a question of service, charity, tolerance, a giving of time, in sympathy and often in most extraordinarily difficult circumstances.

I want each of you to feel that your Quest is really in midstream. You have crossed your bridge, you have more or less given up all things to follow the New Age. To be a new world server, is to be prepared to undertake, in your personal state or measure, wherever you work, live, travel or are, that from now on you are working for GOD, for HIS Universe, for the future of the human race. You are not merely working for your food, your rent, or your comfort.

It is an extraordinary thing, that once you begin to free yourself from the power of possessions, possessions will come to you because you can be trusted with them. And that may surprise some of you. Often I hear people say, 'If only we won the football pools, what we would not do!' But that is a very cheap form of charity, though it may be very nice to have sleepless nights getting rid of it. If that is the state of our charity, then we have not gone very far. There is somebody's key that does not fit the lock; there are old folk down the road who could do with a bunch of flowers because that means that someone cares, and not all the money in the world could give them that same assurance. You may be tired and want to watch your television, but it would be very nice to go and baby-sit for nothing, and let someone go out for a change and get to know themselves better. There are many ways in which we can do things, and it is in these details, in the small items of service, that the new world is being born.

Feel now, as we come to the end of this cycle of preparation and training, that not a word has been wasted, not a statement has gone unnoticed. That the deep subconscious could recite every word that has been said, that in character and nature, are waiting potentialities to manifest not only life, but to change the hungers and needs of other people. Gold and silver we may not have, but if we can say, 'Take up your bed and walk!' then our Quest will have been on right and true lines, for it is here we must decide. Do you remember that parable in the Bible which tells the story of the wedding feast? The guests were invited and the feast was ready, when one by one the excuses came in. 'I'm moving into a new house.' 'My daughter is getting married.' 'I must go and bury my aunt.' 'My vineyard wants watering.' 'I must visit a distant relative,' and so on, until there was not a guest left. Then—'Go out into the highways and by-ways and bring in all the beggars, the lame, the old, the blind, bring them in and let them share the feast.' You are the feast, each one of you, and if you ask the mighty and the great, you will get nowhere, but if you seek amongst the hungry and under-nourished, among those who have lost their way upon the path-way of life, then you can become as a Way to those people. Then your life will not have been wasted, you will not have lived in vain, but the whole of the history of the future will bear the impression of your character, your giving, your life. Feel every day that the Quest is new. Every morning wake and start the day, say, "Today is a day of Quest and Adventure. I do not know what is to happen, whom I am to meet, what will be said. It is an unwritten page, it is something which is start-lingly new, challenging and unexpected." Then go into that day with a sense of excitement and wonder, and realize that every person met, will not be by accident. Every letter written, every thought, every action, will be a part of life's evolution unfold-ing itself. No longer is any action trivial. Nothing is bad or good luck. It is all a part of the unfolding future, unveiling itself in our daily life, and giving, our daily Quest. Seen like this, every day can be an adventure and following the ways of the Spirit. Yours will be the voice of the Comforter, yours the touch that heals, you will be an instrument of the new world. Feel this, know this, and never lose sight of it, and you will find that your hungers, your needs, will be met, and met in such abundance that you will be trusted to have much left over to feed and nourish many others.

138

MEDITATION

Let us feel the Quest as a constant state of union, a state of Being in which each one of us must be alive, keen and aware to fulfil each living moment. Into this silence pour yourself, your sorrows, your hopes, your future; pour every regret, every shame, every guilt, every promise, every hope. Pour them literally out upon Heaven's floor and say, "Of these I will have no more. Only of that which is of the Heavens, the heights, the unfolding splendour, the hidden glory, this is my quest and for this will I live."

CHAPTER THIRTEEN

The Attainment

When we come to those stages in which the Soul is in a state of continual unveiling, it is well we appreciate that the moment of re-birth is when we realize that we are Beings beyond our own capacity, that we have an in-born personality which far exceeds our human limitations and that the qualities within the Soul-force are a living record of our past, present and future. We are over-inclined to fix our gaze on the expression of physical force, but there comes a time when every Initiate and seeker on the Path has to turn away from the force of physical expression and to use mind and Soul-force. Once we see that the Soul-force and mind are the actual projected partners in which the creativity of new patterns is being formed, we can then remove the brake of physical limitation and realize Soul-mind force as expansion. It is in this tremendous realm of the expansionist field that the esoteric teaching slowly but surely takes its students and Initiates into a new world which has entirely different foundations from those previously known. These foundations are very necessary at different times in our lives but foundations must change as the structure changes and become strengthened and streamlined and able to take the stresses and strains with which the mind force involves the human force.

Therefore, we need a constant change in pattern by which the personality involved within the so-called conflict of life becomes an extended force which takes hold of the Karmic foundations of every individual life and literally shakes them to their very depths. In fact, many who first touch this inward or deeper knowledge are almost afraid that the revelation will prove too much or that they will have to renounce old foundations and traditions, even religious foundations as well.

Truth is indeed to set us free; it is the difference between attainment and the bondage of slavery and we have a choice between being a slave to worn-out creeds or being a person whose freedom is a part of a new 'texture' of thinking and living. It is said, and with some truth, that pure love is based on non-attachment. When we realize that this question of attachment to things is part of the living force of human existence, we naturally find ourselves exposed to contests between personality ownership and the desire of the Soul-force to set us free. The conflict between the possessional love of the human Being and the free love of the Soul Being acts as a spur and sets up its own contrasting forces as well. But we must not see this as competition, that is only for the lesser primitive forces still evolving by the trial and error process. But the Initiates have reached that stage when need for trial and error ceases and they enter into the path of attainment which is by non-action. This sounds as if we are not participating, for non-attachment and non-doing seem at first a lazy man's philosophy of living, but it takes more discipline not to do something—it requires more courage to be non-attached, than it does to sell ourselves to a picture image or religious doctrine or some fixation which soothsays our fears away. These latter are a state of sleep, while the former is an intense state of Soul-force at work, and is actually changing our foundations.

In this we extend beyond time-consciousness which, in limiting our horizons, is again a human force belonging to the primitive field of attachments; but as time is an element—not a force but merely an element, just as electricity or air or gas or gravity—we begin to see that we can be imprisoned in an element or we can flow freely. This is the wonderful, exhilarating fact—that once we can get rid of the astral, the psyche and the mental forces which restrict the expansion of the human consciousness, we can set a goal and see a beacon; this is a mountain worth scaling if we only have the courage to free ourselves from the chains, the bonds and the forces by which our temporary patterns have been shaped.

Now let us see where non-attachment really takes us. This idea of being possessed or possessing represents perhaps to the main human family its basic pattern of security; and here we are coming along with a philosophy which attacks the basic force of the family—the human pattern. Truth is strangled by this possessional force with its resistance to change and its upholding of the fixed systems which obliterate the Soul's endeavours. The relationship between the mind and the Soul is something to which every seeker on the Path must give full consideration and rise above the conflict of human doubts, fears and uncertainties—birth, death, survival, and Karma, for interesting as they once were, they have now completed their purpose. We need no longer belong to those areas of superstitious darkness for we are entering into the era of the known, where the man who has this knowledge is different from the man who exists in self-ignorance. How deliberately self-ignorant are we? It is only by direct experience that we suddenly catch a glimpse of ourselves reacting, responding, in a combative, retaliatory way to the conduct of others; we realize then that we are still very deeply rooted in our past and it needs a tremendous spiritual effort to break these chains of the primitive instincts and so release the Soul forces. We must not fritter these forces into the fear-fields of death, disease, disaster, unemployment, insecurity, and sleepless nights; all these are fears of bereavement—there is no bereavement in a living force.

Continuity of consciousness knows no death—it merely experiences the changing of form consciousness—so life is not a matter of life and death any more, it is a continuous flow. It is the force of Soul and mind flowing into consciousness at different levels, all at the same and wonderful time.

We now realize that the evolutionary pattern of attainment is going on at many levels and fields, all at the same time, that people appear to do less in the physical sense—providing they are using their mind-force and not sitting about in a state of semi-sleep—and are able to manifest on dimensions not imprisoned in time. Here is the power factor. Where, before, we relied entirely upon a physical energy force to alter or change a sequence or a series of effects, we now find that mind and Soul force in action can change and raise it. We see this in illness, and in the therapeutic side of the esoteric work, this ability to change the foundation, to free the consciousness, to heighten the expansion. To remove the fear and to set the Soul free upon its Path, is of paramount importance. This is the essence of healing taught in all esoteric schools and foundations.

Now the Soul force is a discriminating, not a slave, force and spiritual discrimination is very essential. Every seeker, every Initiate, will eventually develop this for himself by challenge and exposure. Some do not like this exposure, it demands too much of the Soul, but we can see that we waste three parts of an earthly life on self-interest, self-power, and we must change the emphasis to mind-Soul power. Then, and only then, all that energy force and power, which was frittered away in sweat, tears, sorrow, tragedy, woe and fear, is raised into its true concept and now becomes Soul-force in action, dynamic and splendid.

Naturally, as we study the various systems of the religious faiths of the world, we use this sense of discrimination. We change, or try to change, many of our fundamental foundations and, at the same time, we endeavour to reach into other dimensions, each time trying to qualify or release some part of the hidden personality into an entirely new field. One can sense the sadness of a faith, a religion or doctrine which has lost its power force, its Soul force, and is living in a state of repetitional inertia, giving out its platitudes and handing out its half-truths, but doing very little in Soul activity.

If we belong to these particular sects we are required to surrender our will, our discrimination—surely too big a price, just to find a temporary security in a pattern which is almost Soulless. We need the full invigoration of the mind-Soul force if the personality is to be instrumental in creating the world which the Soul is capable of producing. So powerful is this that even the transmutation of cell tissue of the body becomes a normal thing. The impossible becomes the ordinary, and again we begin to enter into a dimension of creativeness which surpasses the wildest imagination of those who are imprisoned in the personality life force and know no other. This is perhaps more noticeable by comparison. One begins to find that the old does not fit into the new, and let us be grateful for that. Our friends are beginning to bore us and we look for another kind of personality in people. The type of book we used to read no longer holds us; interest in certain things seems to wane, it has no flavour and we begin to feel the sense of reflection, a realization of another power force in action beside the characteristic behaviour of a human being. This is getting to Soul level exchange, where we are feeling into the deep personality of a person instead of being concerned with the outward show.

Naturally, we shall in the course of this eliminating contest of life, have to weed out many factors by which the body is torturing us, though most of the torture is purely the difference between self-ignorance and self-knowing. When we are self-knowing, we can take all of life's medicine in a non-attached way because it does not hurt us any more. But if we are over-immersed into the attachment of possessions everything will hurt us. The complete separation which takes place at the re-birth of the Soul, when we leave everything behind and are not allowed to take anything with us—even to the first stage of the astral—the stripping clean at the passing of Soul-force consciousness to another plane, this should not be the wrench, the rupture it is. We should see to it that this is a process of natural birth beginning to take place, long before our assignment in Time has been completed and that we are unattached through the pure love of realization, so that whatever we do and wherever we are, we live as a free entity instead of as a bonded serf or a possessed personality. We are all aware of the possessed personality. One is not with them for very long before the words 'I' and 'my' dominate and one realizes there is no other world to these personalities except their own self-interest—self-survival, which at one time, we may have thought was the ideal way to live, but gradually as our expansion takes place, we find that it is not. It is on that measure, that note, that one notices those who are in the attainment cycle, who are shedding their primitive pasts and entering into the new concepts, new dimensions and new worlds. For this is a New world of mind and Soul-force, it is not a world of possession, nor of ownership, it is a world of intense awareness and freedom.

Many people are afraid of freedom because it means that they may have to stand on their own initiative, and take responsibility for their own actions. They will have to live by direct experimentation instead of being told, regimented or cared for from the cradle to the grave, in the state of the sleep-walker who is afraid to awaken. If you have any doubt about this, try self-observation. When you are going through a particularly exposing experience, instead of letting the experience carry you, use a detached observation and watch the reactions of your human personality against the background of your spiritual knowing. You may see a contrast which is not always pleasant. On the one hand, we seem to think we have attained quite a degree of spiritual freedom, or a certain level of quality of thinking, then suddenly we are exposed to some direct physical experience affecting the personality, and it is here the courage of the seeker on the Path is needed more than anywhere else.

Another of the various levels of attainment is what we call the acceptance of the evolving principle, and this perhaps is one of the most difficult things to accustom oneself to. People often say, "If there is a GOD, why is this person suffering so? If there is a GOD, why is this allowed to go on?" and so on. It seems there is a general acceptance that everything bad is blamed on GOD, and everything good is taken for granted as some sort of personal satisfaction or attainment. GOD gets only the blame and never the praise! Only recently a person asked me why a certain man should be taken at the height of his career. I had to gently point out that picture-images are bad for everyone and almost every great Soul, having achieved its mission—makes a dramatic exit. Few of the founders of great religions or schools of thought have died in their beds. No!

They all paid the price of the moment of realization, the moment of Truth, and if we go through the various religions, and history itself, we shall find the pioneers, the forefront thinkers the doers, all those who were ahead of their time, leaders, inspired from the great Hierarchy of world leadership, all of them expect to leave this plane in some unusual way.

Instead of seeing life in a continual sense of tragedy, a war with GOD, the Initiate looks at these things much more deeply and sees that they originated before this earth life. This happening is prophecy come true, this is a moment of great truth. This is not an afflicted child that we are seeing, nor ill fortune or bad luck that we are witnessing, this is not tragedy, but the great mystery of the evolved event, working out its dramatic pattern, its lesson of experience in fullness of time. When this affects other people, we can see it in a more remote way, but when this thing touches us personally it needs a tremendous digging into our depths, our foundations, to be able to hold on to the higher personality of our realistic teachings and then apply them to this issue, at this time.

Here then, we cease competing with the Almighty, and try to see that the changing world should only alter through guiding movements and not by a series of impacts and collisions whereby crises follow crises, and in which the world itself becomes involved in chaos. There is no accident, no casual event; there is only this wonderful pre-time, and it is in this pre-timing of the manifest to the un-manifest that each one of us has personal experience, because even the length of our time on earth is pre-destined. We prepared the fall of Cain, we entered into very close relationships with each other before we arrived here and the pattern of history was fitted into our past Karma and capacity. Each moment of birth fits into the very movement of the Stars in space; we are a Cosmos in action, not only the Solar past but the Cosmic; and these things are all timed to a human birth, to human life and bent.

We begin to see the majesty, the magnificence, the tremendous unfolding wonder of this fulfilling force within the Soul and mind and as we move into this new dimension, we must be prepared not only to renounce the old foundations, change the old faiths and beliefs, but be prepared to become New Age Servers, World Servers, instead of a family servant or slave. Even the Lord Christ had to send His human mother about her business because He had His Heavenly Father's business to attend to; so if it sometimes means conflict with family, we must feel this as an inevitable thing—not to go to war with it, but to see it through in a gracious and kindly way with a deep compassion. One who is on the Path of attainment must learn to change judgment to compassion, for we shall find that many things with which before we were at war or in conflict, now have a deep human feeling and call for spiritual respect or reverence.

Now, we must realize that the Spirit which projects itself through the Soul-mind also has a waiting force. This is a rather interesting level because where previously the Soul-mind force dealt a great deal with knowledge, the Spirit force, which works through the Soul, does not; it deals with its own deep sense of knowing. In fact, there is no such thing as learning, there is only unveiling; their is self-recognition, self-realization, self-knowing. The difference is that mind-Soul force is one which works through the intellect and the intuition, manifesting the natural laws— while the Spirit force is entirely as inspirational-intuitional force. When we meet people who are able to do this—and not many can—we find that their thinking life does not think! We all get rather fed-up with a thinking life which will not stop thinking! It goes chattering on, keeping us awake at night, and we cannot control it. It seems to run away with its own tail and taking us through all its horrors and tortures and its "never-lie-down-ness." Then suddenly it stops and we stop using the power of mind force to build up a relationship or knowledge; we now begin to use the storehouse of the Universe instead of trying to use the pitiful storehouse of mind relationship.

On the one hand we have only what we attained in the school of knowledge; on the other, we have the great reservoir of wisdom and power which already exists beyond knowledge. This may seem a little difficult, that no sooner do we reach one stage of attainment than we immediately sense another one ahead of it. But this is attainment, it is a "going-on-ness," a continuous spiral from one state of consciousness into the challenge and the excitement of another.

Occasionally, we get glimpses of this Spirit force, almost of an inborn intelligence, answering our questions even before we have asked them. Sometimes we let the phenomena of the event work through its cause and effect, without our getting high blood pressure and lying awake all night, allowing the mystery of the event within a timed cause to communicate. This is a great release, a great freedom, and these things we must look at because it is in our relationship to the passing of time to events and movements of history, and in the unfoldment of the true personality, that our future lies, that will decide where we are going and what we shall be.

And so, when we are able to use the Spirit flow of intuitional thinking—in some cases, inspired thinking—this is leadership in action, world leadership, by which we are not dependent upon the human intellect to resolve the conflict or the problems, but the Spirit force that flows from the ALL-knowing, ALL-seeing depths and heights, merging its intuitive feeling into that event or problem and completely transmuting it.

There may only be one or two occasions where this happens in the whole of ones life, but when they do happen, one will never forget them, because they will be moments of such personal truth—unexplainable to other people—something sacred, something to which one will return, dwell on and use time and time again as an unfolding power-mystery, supplying that particular answer, nourishment, encouragement or vision, at the time when it was most needed.

Attainment means compassion, love means non-possession; we must also go into what we term graciousness, which transforms the human personality when we touch these high dimensions. We have mentioned compassion and mercy and love,

148

but here we touch on what we call the graciousness of Soul. This shows itself in a willingness to Be—that is, we do not live by compulsion or duty any more. We act without motive, because we want to and it is in our hearts to do so. No longer have we the whip of punishment by Heaven or hell, or of loss or gain; now, whatever is done is done for the sake of doing—no other reason, no motive, and certainly not gain, but for this wonderful art of doing for doing's sake and living for the sake of living! This makes for a gentle graciousness of temperament, a cheerfulness, a wholesomeness, a cleanliness, a forthrightness; the difference between a person who is out in the front living their own life, and one who is sitting in the shadow, sulking behind the astral scenes, afraid to come out and meet the full challenge of living. In this wholesomeness and cheerfulness and willingness lies deep compassion and mercy and at the same time we find in our hearts a sense of living which we can transmit to those who are still imprisoned in the physical personalities of force. This then, is the measure of healing because healing is resurrection, is the salvation of a Soul that is lost, the raising of a consciousness which cannot find its signpost, the lifting of the personality into the full consciousness of Soul-Mind-Spirit action.

So, our attainments are what we are; but our attainments of the future are so unlimited, are so great, so wonderful, vast, so magnificent and beautiful, that it passes our imagination to comprehend them. This is the dimension of work and whatever use we can make of this earth at this time will help us to proceed higher on the spiral on earth, than we shall be able to in Heaven, because in Heaven many have achieved much of the greater glory and the inner realization, thus there is not quite the same opportunity as there is in this earth. To attain under these conditions has a very high, lasting and wonderful value. So life at its lowest can be life at its highest! All is the great and wonderful adventure of the human race.

MEDITATION

Let us enter into the full silence; let us dispossess ourselves and as we become in that sense free from the bonds of personality or enslavement, these moments of meditation can reveal to us our state of realization. This we must do every day, constantly, continuously, without ever pausing to think of any effect or promise or reward, to live without motive, for the joy of living, doing and being, in the creative principle of Life.